The New Russian Nationalism

THE WASHINGTON PAPERS

. . . intended to meet the need for an authoritative, yet prompt, public appraisal of the major developments in world affairs.

MANUSCRIPT SUBMISSION

The Washington Papers and Praeger Publishers welcome inquiries concerning manuscript submissions. Please include with your inquiry a curriculum vita, synopsis, table of contents, and estimated manuscript length. Submissions to *The Washington Papers* should be sent to *The Washington Papers*; The Center for Strategic and International Studies; Georgetown University; 1800 K Street NW; Suite 400; Washington, DC 20006. Book proposals should be sent to Praeger Publishers; 521 Fifth Avenue; New York NY 10175.

The Washington Papers/116

The New Russian Nationalism

John B. Dunlop

Foreword by Robert F. Byrnes

Published with The Center for
Strategic and International Studies
Georgetown University, Washington, D.C.

PRAEGER SPECIAL STUDIES • PRAEGER SCIENTIFIC

New York • Philadelphia • Eastbourne, UK
Toronto • Hong Kong • Tokyo • Sydney

Library of Congress Cataloging in Publication Data

Dunlop, John B.
The new Russian nationalism.

(The Washington papers, ISSN 0278-937X ;
vol. xiii, 116)
Published with the Center for Strategic and
International Studies, Georgetown University,
Washington, D.C."
1. Nationalism – Soviet Union – Addresses, essays,
lectures. 2. Soviet Union – Politics and government –
1953– – Addresses, essays, lectures. I. Title.
II. Series.
DK288.D86 1985 947.085 85-12372
ISBN 0-03-006259-4
ISBN 0-03-006262-4 (pbk.)

The *Washington Papers* are written under the auspices of The Center for Strategic and International Studies (CSIS), Georgetown University and published with CSIS by Praeger Publishers. The views expressed in these papers are those of the authors and not necessarily those of the Center.

Published in 1985 by Praeger Publishers
CBS Educational and Professional Publishing, a Division of CBS Inc.
521 Fifth Avenue, New York, NY 10175 USA

56789 052 987654321

Printed in the United States of America on acid-free paper

INTERNATIONAL OFFICES

Orders from outside the United States should be sent to the appropriate address listed below. Orders from areas not listed below should be placed through CBS International Publishing, 383 Madison Ave., New York, NY 10175 USA

Australia, New Zealand
Holt Saunders, Pty, Ltd., 9 Waltham St., Artarmon, N.S.W. 2064, Sydney, Australia

Canada
Holt, Rinehart & Winston of Canada, 55 Horner Ave., Toronto, Ontario, Canada M8Z 4X6

Europe, the Middle East, & Africa
Holt Saunders, Ltd., 1 St. Anne's Road, Eastbourne, East Sussex, England BN21 3UN

Japan
Holt Saunders, Ltd., Ichibancho Central Building, 22-1 Ichibancho, 3rd Floor, Chiyodaku, Tokyo, Japan

Hong Kong, Southeast Asia
Holt Saunders Asia, Ltd., 10 Fl, Intercontinental Plaza, 94 Granville Road, Tsim Sha Tsui East, Kowloon, Hong Kong

Manuscript submissions should be sent to the Editorial Director, Praeger Publishers, 521 Fifth Avenue, New York, NY 10175 USA

Contents

Foreword

U.S. specialists have greatly increased their knowledge and understanding of Russia and the Soviet Union since the great expansion of such studies began at the end of World War II. U.S. policymakers, the informed public, and students of all ages and kinds have thus enjoyed the opportunity to deepen their comprehension of the baffling state and society that threaten the peace and the world's stability.

In our great rush to leap from ignorance and misinformation to the kind of understanding that would enable us to face calmly the problems the Soviets raise or exacerbate, we have naturally concentrated first upon the study of history, literature, the political system, and the economy – in that order. The reasons for these priorities are obvious: these elements play an important role in the Soviet system, as well as in the United States, and in our universities those disciplines for the study of other countries and cultures have been among the strongest. Analyses in these fields, which provided the bases from which we view the Soviet Union, have therefore flourished and created a distorted frame of reference.

Meanwhile, the study of other aspects of Soviet life has trailed. Only in recent years have such central, but less available and traditional, elements as philosophy, science, education, religion, and nationalism begun to attract the attention required for a balanced and full analysis of the Soviet Union. U.S. scholars in the pragmatic tradition have traditionally neglected the study of philosophy, and science is a second, neglected culture for nonscientists. U.S. scholars generally pay little attention to education or to institutional history, thus we also neglect them in our studies of the Soviet Union. Nationalism and even patriotism have declined sharply in the United States and in the Western world, especially among intellectuals, since 1945. Most observers have welcomed this because of the destructive role nationalism has played in Europe in the twentieth century and because international instruments or approaches seem more promising agents for peace and progress than the national state. In addition, few scholars have deep religious convictions, and religion seems a spent force in the Western world, except as the cause of especially thorny and destructive conflict in areas such as Ireland and Cyprus and for the much-ridiculed fundamentalists. U.S. scholars and the public they represent have consequently neglected both religion and nationalism in their analyses of the Soviet Union.

Professor Dunlop is one of the handful of immensely able scholars who understand the role religion and nationalism have played throughout Russian history, the vital position Marxism-Leninism occupied as a kind of religion until it ebbed at every level below that at the top – where it remains the essential legitimizing force – and the new stirrings of religion and nationalism of the last two decades. This volume supplements his 1983 volume, *The Faces of Contemporary Russian Nationalism*, by relating developments in the most recent years to that fundamental base. It represents the same careful scholarship that one finds in the most objective analyses of other aspects of Soviet life, although it deals with information even more fragile and subject to misinterpretation than Soviet economic statistics. His analyses of movies are especially fruitful – the appearances of Russian nationalism in mass media are truly representative: they reflect what those making films wish to produce, what the regime allows or even encourages, and what millions of viewers appreciate and enjoy. Analysis of these films and of journals, of the government's policies toward the ideas they present, and of *samizdat* publications provides a vivid description of cultural-political developments of enormous importance. Dunlop's conclusions about the significance of the rise of Russian nationalism and his suggestions for Western policy, especially that of Western radios, should stir interest among everyone interested in the Soviet Union and in international politics. This is truly an exciting book.

Robert F. Byrnes
Distinguished Professor of History
Indiana University

Acknowledgments

I would like to dedicate this book to my parents, John T. and Dorothy Dunlop, with affection and gratitude. I should also like to thank the following scholars who commented upon the various drafts of the essays contained in this paper: L. H. Gann, Alexis Klimoff, Leopold Labedz, Peter Reddaway, and Nicholas V. Riasanovsky. It goes without saying that the responsibility for the final text is mine alone.

About the Author

John B. Dunlop received his B.A., *magna cum laude*, from Harvard and his M.A. and Ph.D. from Yale. He was a professor and department chairman at Oberlin College before becoming, in 1983, associate director and senior fellow at the Hoover Institution, Stanford University. He is the author of *The New Russian Revolutionaries* (1976) and *The Faces of Contemporary Russian Nationalism* (1983) and coeditor of *Aleksandr Solzhenitsyn: Critical Essays and Documentary Materials* (1973) and *Solzhenitsyn in Exile* (forthcoming, 1985). He has published numerous essays in such journals as *Survey, Soviet Studies*, and *The Times Literary Supplement*. He is currently researching a book on Soviet film of the post-Stalin period.

The New Russian Nationalism

Introduction

Russian nationalism has consistently played a large part in modern Russian history. Yet Western analysts have only recently begun to note the marked growth in what might be called the new Russian nationalism of the Brezhnev and post-Brezhnev period. This omission should cause surprise. Western specialists on Soviet affairs have long taken a considerable interest in the nationalism of minority peoples in the USSR, yet the nationalism of the largest and the most significant ethnic group, the Russians, has received short shrift. The emergence of Aleksandr Solzhenitsyn as a clear-cut nationalist in the early 1970s and the unmistakable appearance of strong Russian nationalist sympathies among various Soviet elites during the Brezhnev years have finally occasioned an awakening on the part of Western analysts.

In late 1983, I published a book, *The Faces of Contemporary Russian Nationalism*,* devoted to the rise of Russian nationalism in the post-Stalin period. Since the completion of the manuscript upon which that study was based, important political changes have occurred in the Soviet Union,

*John B. Dunlop, *The Faces of Contemporary Russian Nationalism* (Princeton, N.J.: Princeton University Press, 1983).

most notably the deaths of Leonid Brezhnev and Mikhail Suslov and the accessions of Iurii Andropov, Konstantin Chernenko, and Mikhail Gorbachev. These events (only briefly alluded to in a postscript to *Faces*) have inevitably, and at times dramatically, affected the fortunes of contemporary Russian nationalism.

Part one of the present collection consists of three essays that focus upon the "Russian nationalist controversy" as it simmered and occasionally boiled up under the Andropov and Chernenko leaderships. A fourth essay deals with the question of what the West's policies should be toward the Russian nationalists. The three essays constituting part two treat noteworthy political, cultural, and religious developments of the mid-to-late Brezhnev period.

An introduction to these essays calls for a consideration of certain fundamental questions connected with an accurate assessment of contemporary Russian nationalism. The most critical of these concerns is the political importance of the nationalists. How politically powerful are they? Given the closed nature of Soviet society in general, and of elite circles in particular, this is not an easy question to answer. A response requires considerable detective work on the part of the researcher. The seven essays constituting this volume – as well as my earlier book – produce strong evidence of mass sympathy for Russian nationalist causes. This sympathy contrasts sharply with the demonstrable widespread erosion of support for the official ideology, Marxism-Leninism. Whether one is speaking of mass voluntary societies such as the 37-million-member All-Russian Society for the Preservation of Nature[1] or the 14.7-million-member All-Russian Society for the Preservation of Historical and Cultural Monuments[2], or of the 50-million-member Russian Orthodox Church[3], one is dealing with mass organizations whose members exhibit marked sympathy for Russian nationalist issues. Major cultural events, such as the 1978 and 1979 Moscow and Leningrad exhibits of paintings by nationalist artist Il'ia Glazunov, also provide convincing evidence of such broad-based support. (These exhibits are discussed in several of the essays contained in the collection.)

The Soviet regime has not traditionally chosen to respond to the desires of its populace, and it can therefore be argued that Soviet mass sentiment is politically almost irrelevant. If, however, Russian nationalism were to enjoy significant support among Soviet elites, its political prospects would increase. The essays contained in this collection demonstrate the existence of such support. To quantify this support and to assess its intensity is virtually impossible, given the closed nature of Soviet society. The concern exhibited by the Andropov and Chernenko regimes over elite support for Russian nationalism is, however, an important indicator that the Soviet leadership takes the phenomenon seriously. If the regime does, we should too.

How much importance should be ascribed to the various strands of contemporary Russian nationalism? In the final essay of this collection, I attempt a typology of current Russian nationalism and seek to assess the strength of its various strands. Even the extreme and bizarre views of certain nationalist spokesmen – for example, the *Mnogaia leta* (Many Years) authors discussed in chapter 7 – should not automatically be relegated by Western readers to the fringe of Soviet society. The Bolshevik Revolution hurled a largely peasant-based, traditional society into 65 years of perhaps unprecedented social dislocation and upheaval. Soviet society today has few parallels with that of the contemporary West. To engage in "mirror-imaging" is incorrect and dangerous when dealing with such a dissimilar society as the USSR. It takes not only a great deal of study but also leaps of empathy and intuitive imagination to begin to comprehend the intellectual and political life of the present-day Soviet Union.

In chapter 4 of this collection, I move from description and analysis to policy recommendations. The following represents the conceptual underpinning for these recommendations:

1. From its inception the Soviet Union has been an ideocracy. As Martin Malia has shown in a fine series of lec-

tures on the Russian Revolution and its aftermath, since the late 1930s, the USSR has been, of necessity, an expansionist power; expansion is part of the "genetic code" of the Soviet system.[4] The West confronts an unremitting threat in the form of this metastasizing ideocracy.

2. It is incorrect and foolhardy to regard the USSR as a traditional nation-state; indeed no Communist regime can be so regarded. There are, to be sure, continuities between pre and postrevolutionary Russia, but the discontinuities are of far greater significance. In Alain Besançon's words, the USSR is an *imitatio perversa* of tsarist Russia, just as, for example, the German Democratic Republic has a perverse, pseudomorphic relationship to Prussian tradition and Maoist China to Chinese imperial ceremony.[5] It is its thralldom to ideology that makes the USSR a global threat. Were the USSR to revert to being a traditional nation-state pursuing national objectives, it would be a major improvement from the point of view of the West's vital interests.[6]

3. Because ideology represents the key to Soviet expansion, the West, as a simple act of self-preservation, should seek to put pressure on that ideology, to break off from it the peoples of the USSR, especially the politically dominant ethnic Russians.

4. If it were to pursue such a goal, the West would be helped immeasurably by the fact that Marxism-Leninism has lost its élan and become a "dead" ideology. A dead ideology is most vulnerable.

5. Among both ethnic Russians and non-Russians, nationalism and religio-nationalism are the most powerful forces moving in to fill the vacuum created by the death of Marxist-Leninist ideology.[7]

6. The principal means by which the West can establish contact with the Soviet masses and with Soviet elites is through the foreign radio. Technological advances promise to make television broadcasting to the USSR feasible in the near future. The examples of Czecholslovakia in 1968 and Poland in the early 1980s show that when foreign radio stations succeed in addressing the critical national concerns of

a given people, their broadcasts can help effect change in Communist countries. Up until now, Russian-language broadcasts to the Soviet Union have only been cautiously addressing the national and religio-national needs of ethnic Russians.[8]

A major objection to the above six points is that a Russian nationalist government is likely to be worse than the present ideocratic regime. In company with Besançon, the author considers this objection ill-founded.[9] Whatever its limitations – and they are many – authoritarianism is clearly preferable to ideocracy. Franco's Spain eventually gave birth to a democracy; no Communist regime has as yet done so.

There are, to conclude, unsentimental realpolitik reasons to prefer a nationalist accession to a continuation of the present expansionist ideocracy. In light of the USSR's immense social, demographic, and economic difficulties, a Russian nationalist government would be forced to look inward rather than outward in the direction of external expansion. The removel of Marxist-Leninist legitimacy would also require a nationalist government to accommodate the ethnic strivings of the minority peoples of the USSR and the national goals of the countries of Eastern Europe. Any attempt to apply the White Army slogan of a "single, indivisible Russia" would result in the disintegration of the Soviet empire.

I hope that the essays in this volume will prompt other specialists to devote attention to a major, yet still understudied, political and cultural phenomenon.

Part I

1

Andropov and the Russian Nationalists*

The last years of Brezhnev's reign witnessed a marked rise in the power and influence of the so-called Russian party (*russkaia partiia*). The 100th anniversary of Dostoevskii's death in 1981 represented perhaps the high-water mark of the Russian party's attempts to affect and alter the present and future direction taken by the USSR; in a series of articles using Dostoevskii and his writings as a springboard for Aesopian and not-so-Aesopian reflections, its adherents advanced a number of novel theses concerning the 60 years of Soviet power. These articles appeared in periodicals dominated by Russian nationalists, journals such as *Nash sovremennik* and *Sever*.

What is the Russian party? It is not an organization and not, strictly speaking, a movement. Rather it consists of a great number of individuals whose beliefs range from a Christian variety in the Solzhenitsyn mold to a version of neofascism, but all of whom contend that the Soviet Union must pay more heed to the vital needs and concerns of the most numerous national group, ethnic Russians. (Most ad-

*This essay is a slightly revised version of a paper presented at the Kennan Institute for Advanced Russian Studies, Washington, D.C., January 11, 1984.

herents of the Russian party, incidentally, are what might be called polycentric nationalists, i.e., they hold that all peoples have the right to flourish culturally, linguistically, and religiously.) The higher one ascends the ladder of the political hierarchy, the more one tends to encounter the so-called National Bolshevik strand of Russian nationalism, a statist form of Bolshevism largely shorn of its international or Marxist elements, one for which Fedor Dostoevskii and Vladimir Ilich Lenin, Aleksandr Suvorov and Georgii Zhukov can all serve equally as church fathers. Further away from the political empyrean, one encounters the Christian, Slavophile variant, which has little sympathy for 1917 and its consequences.

During the late 1970s and through the year 1981, the principal vehicle for the expression of the views and core sentiments of the Russian party was the writings of the so-called *derevenshchiki* (village prose writers), especially authors such as the late Fedor Abramov, Valentin Rasputin, Vasilii Belov, Viktor Astaf'ev, and Vladimir Soloukhin. The central sounding board for their ideas was the journal *Nash sovremennik*, which played a role in this period roughly comparable to that of *Molodaia gvardiia* in the late 1960s.[10] The role of belles lettres in contemporary Soviet politics has been pivotal here. Literature and literary criticism have served the Russian party as a means to score telling political points as well as for the projection of alternative models of social development. It is worth noting that, due to the apparent difficulty that the *derevenshchiki* represent to many Western observers, their bold journalistic efforts have not attracted the kind of attention that, for instance, was accorded to the group gathered around *Novyi mir* in the 1960s. What the *derevenshchiki* had to say, however, was every bit as striking.

One example of such unorthodox writing would be Vladimir Shubkin's "The Ever-Burning Bush," an essay published at the end of 1981 in *Nash sovremennik* and devoted to the 100th anniversary of Dostoevskii's death.[11] In his article, Shubkin fully endorses Dostoevskii's focus upon "moral problems" and excoriates any attempt to resolve social problems without primary reference to the moral dimension of those problems. Shubkin allies himself with the efforts of the *derevenshchiki* and singles out such writers as Rasputin, Belov, and Sergei Zalygin for praise. He makes little attempt to conceal his Christian convictions and underlines the traditional historical link between Russia and Orthodox Christianity. One of Shubkin's aims appears to be to shore up the nuclear Russian family, and he believes that the "primal sources of morality" can be traced to the fast-disappearing Russian village.

Shubkin finds little to praise in 60 years of Soviet power. The ideological fanaticism and incitement to hatred of the early Bolsheviks is vehemently rejected. He assails "Maoist ideas of barracks communism" and "the rationalistic style of thinking." Russia, he recalls, was ravaged by fanatics in the late 1920s and 1930s who wanted to throw the nineteenth century Russian classics overboard from the "ship of modernity." Unfortunately, he suggests, the heirs of these extremists remain active today. He discovers "recrudescences of a nihilistic attitude toward the fatherland's culture" among his present-day opponents, a reference to those who would tear down ancient churches and other cultural monuments. Going further, he castigates those who are "completely absorbed in the specifics of various professions, in the technology of production, etc.," a blow aimed at Soviet technocrats, who deride the Russian nationalists' preservationist and ecological concerns as standing athwart the path of expanded Soviet industrial production.

A second example would be R. Gal'tseva and I. Rodnianskaia's essay "*The Brothers Karamazov* as Dostoevskii's Moral Testament," which appeared in the same year in *Sever*.[12] The authors' fervent Orthodox Christian convictions become immediately apparent. For Dostoevskii, they stress, the "moral ideal" *is* the "social ideal." The authors are drawn to the religious idea of "all-oneness" advanced by Dostoevskii and philosopher Vladimir Solov'ev. As for their opponents, the authors hint at a link between the ideas of such individuals and the Grand Inquisitor's "enslavement of conscience." Dostoevskii's testament, they conclude, "is now addressed to us. . . ."

Halfway between such overt Christian views and those of the National Bolsheviks is a piece by Anatolii Znamenskii entitled "The Truth of Life is the Truth of Art," devoted to the writings of *derevenshchik* Vasilii Belov, which appeared in an earlier issue of *Sever.*[13] Znamenskii assails the "great break" (*perelom*) represented by collectivization, which destroyed the traditional Russian village and its mores. In addition to the pernicious path of Trotskyite "voluntarism," he notes, there also existed the way of "Leninist cooperativism." "The people," he insists, "must remember the lessons of the past," and he criticizes the "lack of rebellion" on the part of the victims of collectivization. The heirs of the extremists of the 1920s and 1930s, he intimates, are still at work today.

Vadim Kozhinov's 1981 essay "And Every Tongue Will Name Me . . . " is a National Bolshevik statement that aroused considerable controversy.[14] The article employs the Dostoevskii anniversary as a pretext for developing certain ideas formulated by the influential Soviet scholar Lev Gumilev and earlier by the "Eurasian" school. "The Russian idea," Kozhinov asserts, is different from the "Christian idea," but it is also, he suggests, different from that of Marxism-Leninism. The Russians and non-Russians who inhabit the USSR always have been and are "brothers." The Russian federation of peoples is, happily, free of the ethnic animosities of Western Europe. Nationalism is good as long as it does not seek to deny the worth of other peoples or try to treat them in "cosmopolitan" fashion; Zionism is cited as an example of wrongful nationalism. Kozhinov offers a peroration on the fourteenth century battle of Kulikovo Field, which he sees, oddly, as a decisive struggle between the "multinational Russian state" and an "aggressive cosmopolitan armada," representing the "dark forces" of the world at that time. It is Kozhinov's clear intention to warn of the existence of such an armada today.

One wonders how articles such as these four were able to be published. After all, they are noticeably bolder than the pieces that appeared in *Molodaia gvardiia* in the late 1960s and resulted in the Politburo crackdown of November 1970.

The available evidence suggests that Mikhail Suslov, the

guardian of ideological orthodoxy, served in the last years of his life as a powerful protector for those Russian nationalists who sought to work within the political system to achieve their aims. At some point in the mid-to-late 1970s, Suslov, who reportedly supported the mini-purge of *Molodaia gvardiia* in 1970, became a sympathizer and protector of the Russian party.[15] We know, for example, that he was the shadowy guarantor of Il'ia Glazunov's Manezh exhibit in 1978 (which attracted 600 thousand visitors in a month's time) and of the artist's month-long Leningrad showing in 1979 (which drew approximately 1 million viewers).[16] It also seems that it was Suslov who permitted Gennadii Shimanov's *samizdat* almanac *Mnogaia leta* to appear in 1980 and 1981, the first time since 1974 that a nationalist unofficial publication had not been harassed into nonexistence by the secret police.[17]

Suslov's protection and support for the nationalists were a noteworthy development. It is generally recognized that his power was comparable to, and in some ways greater than, that of General Secretary Leonid I. Brezhnev. To quote historian Roy Medvedev: "In the Central Committee he [Suslov] directed such departments as ideology, agitation and propaganda, science, secondary and tertiary education, and foreign sections. He controlled political education in the Soviet Army and Central Committee information. . . . The Ministry of Culture, the State Committee for the Cinema, and the media organization Gostelradio all operated under his authority. The whole of the press, the censorship, TASS, CPSU contacts with other communist parties, even the USSR's foreign policy —all this lay under his jurisdiction.[18]

Why should Suslov have chosen to play the role of protector vis-à-vis the nationalists? One suspects that the obvious decline in the appeal of the official ideology to the populace was one of the factors behind Suslov's decision. The comment books for Glazunov's exhibits, which have been published in the West, show conclusively the lack of resonance of Marxism-Leninism among the populace and the strong attraction of Russian nationalist themes and sentiments. (An important recent survey of Soviet readership tastes, conducted by the late Klaus Mehnert with the permission of the authorities—and probably of Suslov himself—also confirms this.[19]) The canny Suslov may have been investigating the possibility of a National Bolshevik line of development, a change of no mean significance. In any case, Suslov's protection of the nationalists was impressive, and he shielded writer Vladimir Soloukhin and his heretical views from harsh attacks appearing in *Znamia* and *Nauka i religiia* during 1981.[20]

Suslov's death in January 1982 helped open the gates to Iurii Andropov's ultimately successful bid for power. Equally significant, it allowed opponents of the nationalists, who had been fuming in their impotence, finally to have at the Russian party. From the beginning, Andropov showed himself to be a determined enemy of the Russian nationalists. Standing with him were Soviet technocrats and Marxist-Leninist purists.

Only days after Suslov's death, two brutal attacks rained down on the nationalists: a letter in the ideologically infallible *Kommunist* severely criticizing Soloukhin and the editorial and party committees of *Nash sovremennik* for publishing what were obvious religious meditations (Soloukhin's alleged "flirtation with dear little god" (*zaigryvanie s bozhen'koi*), and, on February 1, an article in *Pravda*, entitled "Preciseness of Criteria," directed at Kozhinov's piece in *Nash sovremennik*, which has already been discussed.[21] The author of the *Pravda* diatribe, V. Kuleshov, assailed a number of self-styled interpreters of Dostoevskii for their "departures from the traditions of Marxist-Leninist esthetics." Kozhinov's views on Kulikovo Field were termed "blasphemous" by Kuleshov, and Marxist-Leninist purism was firmly and resolutely proclaimed in opposition to the revisionism and heresies of the Russian nationalists.

During the 10 months separating the deaths of Suslov and Brezhnev, the Russian party was subjected to blow after blow. The chairman of State Security apparatus, the KGB, in this period was, of course, Andropov (until May), and he then became Suslov's replacement as ideological chieftain. In the short period that he was head of the KGB, Vitalii

Fedorchuk, too, gained the reputation of a relentless persecutor of the Russian nationalists.

After Suslov's death, the security forces launched a severe crackdown on dissenting Russian nationalists. Leonid Borodin and Anatolii Ivanov-Skuratov, both of whom had sympathizers among the National Bolsheviks, were arrested and tried.[22] Natal'ia Lazareva of the Orthodox women's organization, the Maria Club, was seized and broken in captivity; she provided the authorities with the names of some 50 persons associated with the club and its work.[23] Nikolai Blokhin and other publishers of Orthodox religious *samizdat* were likewise seized.[24] Official nationalists, too, were given harsh warnings. Soloukhin and the editor of *Nash sovremennik*, Sergei Vikulov, were forced to recant their heresies on the pages of *Kommunist*,[25] while the influential National Bolshevik tribune Sergei Semanov was removed from his post as editor of *Chelovek i zakon* and threatened with a humiliating search of his apartment if he did not voluntarily surrender the writings of Borodin and other dissenting nationalists.[26]

The writer Georgii Vladimov, who was in the USSR at this time, and who is exceptionally well informed about the fortunes of the Russian party, sums up the situation as follows: "The authorities saw the Russian movement . . . as the main danger. They say that Fedorchuk, who did not stay long as head of the KGB, had time to issue an instruction: 'The chief thing is Russian nationalism; the dissidents will come afterwards – those we will take in one night.'"[27]

The culminating point in the campaign against the nationalists was a Central Committee directive issued in late July 1982, with the cumbersome title "Concerning the Creative Links of Literary-Artistic Journals with the Task of Communist Construction." Lengthy summaries of the decree were published in *Pravda* and *Literaturnaia gazeta*.[28] This decree was explicitly directed at the *derevenshchiki* and their supporters and protectors and was intended as a severe warning, if not a knockout blow. The decree insisted upon Marxist-Leninist *chetkost'* (clarity) in literature and literary criticism, both of which, moreover, were to be ruled by the principles of *partiinost'* (party-mindedness) and *narodnost'* (closeness to the people). "Confusion in worldview" and "an inability to examine social phenomena historically, from clear-cut class positions" were sharply denounced. Greater *boevitost'* (combativeness) and *printsipial' nost'* (adhesion to principles) were said to be needed. There should also be more emphasis on the country's current social and economic development and on the formation of a "new man." Soviet literature, the decree underlined, must "march in step with the times" and should provide its readers with "positive heroes" in the hallowed tradition of Socialist Realism. Too much attention, on the other hand, was being devoted to such subjects as "the history of the fatherland, the social revolution, and collectivization." The present, the decree emphasized, outweighs the past. The neo-Stalinist nature of the decree is apparent, as is the hostility toward the *derevenshchiki* and the Russian party.

In December 1982, Andropov made his first major speech after becoming general secretary. The statement was devoted to the sixtieth anniversary of the formation of the USSR, and Andropov notably and noticeably downplayed the role of ethnic Russians in the Soviet federation. He also advanced the highly controversial merger theory (*sliianie*), according to which the peoples of the Soviet Union will merge into one entity, *sovetskii chelovek* (Soviet man).[29] Brezhnev, it should be noted, had carefully avoided this term, no doubt because it had caused considerable trouble for First Party Secretary Nikita Khrushchev earlier.[30]

How does one explain Andropov's fierce hostility toward the Russian party? One can only speculate. He seems to have been a convinced technocrat and believer in the NTR (*nauchno-tekhnicheskaia revoliutsiia*, or "scientific and technical revolution"), vehemently opposed to all nationalisms. If, as many commentators (including Zhores Medvedev[31]) claim, he was not by background an ethnic Russian, his hostility to the Russian nationalists would be even more understandable.

In a paradoxical sense, Brezhnev's death also served to brake Andropov's assault on the nationalists. Although Andropov assumed the post of general secretary, and later added the title of chairman of the presidium of the Supreme Soviet as well, he had to surrender the all-important ideological portfolio to Chernenko, and the latter, while no friend of the nationalists, appears to have inherited some of his mentor, Brezhnev's, caution in dealing with them. In any case, a tapering off in the campaign against the nationalists and their views began in December 1982. Here, as in many other initiatives (such as increased discipline in the workplace), Andropov's momentum seems to have ground to a virtual halt.

A sign that changes were afoot appeared as early as December 5, when nationalist tribune Petr Proskurin published a lyrical essay, "The Cherished Word" (*Slovo zavetnoe*) in *Pravda*.[32] The essay, which directly contradicted what Andropov was to write in the same newspaper two weeks later, is a hymn to the ethnic Russian people and to the "one and undivided" (*edinaia, nedelimaia*—the White army slogan!) family of nations gathered around it. A National Bolshevik, Proskurin accepts the 1917 revolution, but as an expression of the will of the Russian people. His article is replete with references to great battles—Kulikovo Field, Borodino, the Kursk Salient—underlining the mobilizational need for Russian nationalism. A mystical and powerful faith in Russia makes itself felt throughout Proskurin's article.

In January 1983, a final attempt was made to bring the Russian party to heel. A session of the secretariat of the Writer's Union was held to examine the journal *Sever*;[33] the session was attended by such long-time and proven antinationalists as Iurii Surovtsev, Aleksandr Dement'ev, and Feliks Kuznetsov, but by none of the nationalist sympathizers on the secretariat (such as Proskurin, Mikhail Alekseev, or Anatolii Ivanov, the editor of *Molodaia gvardiia*). The purpose of the meeting was to put the July 1982 Central Committee decree into effect through an examination of the journal *Sever*; it was underlined that the lessons learned from this endeavor should be applied to all other Soviet journals. *Sever* was charged with indulging in too much "ethnography," with "unclear abstract and moralizing formulations," and with an "undifferentiated class attitude toward history." The "extra social" analyses of Dostoevskii's writings carried in recent issues of *Sever* were pronounced dangerously wrong. *Sever* was advised to participate actively in "the propaganda of the peace-loving foreign policy of the CPSU [the Communist Party of the Soviet Union]" rather than to immerse itself in the past and was told to attack the USSR's ideological opponents in the West. The decisions of this session were summarized in *Literaturnaia gazeta* but not, significantly, in *Pravda*.

As it turned out, this session of the Writers' Union secretariat was the last gasp in a campaign that ran out of gas when Andropov surrendered the ideological portfolio to Chernenko. Other factors behind the loss of momentum may have been a successful regrouping of Andropov's opponents in the Politburo and, by mid-1983, a serious deterioration in Andropov's health.

What is the present status of the Russian party? Although bloodied by Andropov's assault, it does not seem to have suffered irremediable damage. According to Georgii Vladimov, it has "both protectors and sympathizers" in the Central Committee apparatus.[34] Equally as significant, it enjoys strong support in the military. "I know," Vladimov remarked, "that among the military, basically among the senior officers – majors, lieutenant colonels, and colonels – there are people who think boldly, who understand the necessity of carrying out their national tasks, who are oppressed by the fact that there is not now in Russia a ruling national idea. It is not accidental that at the trial of A. Ivanov-Skuratov it emerged that many of his appeals had been printed on the typewriters of the General Staff. That means that they sympathized with him there. . . ."[35]

In attacking the Russian party openly, and in seeking to suppress it as a tendency, Andropov took a serious political risk. His extremely short reign makes it difficult, however, to assess the extent of that risk. With Andropov's departure from the political scene, the knotty problem of what to do with the nationalists became that of his successor, Konstantin Chernenko.

2

The *Nash Sovremennik* Affair, 1981–1982*

The journal *Nash sovremennik*, a publication of the Russian Socialist Federation of Soviet Republics (RSFSR) Writers' Union, served as a sounding board for Russian nationalist thought and sentiment throughout the Brezhnev period. I have decided to focus upon the 1981 and 1982 runs of the journal for the following reasons: during this period, *Nash sovremennik* began to display the outspokenness and bold qualities of *Molodaia gvardiia* in the late 1960s (an episode that was brought to a halt by a Politburo decision in late 1970); second, 1981 and 1982 were critical years for Russian nationalists and, indeed, for the entire Soviet Union, witnessing as they did the deaths of Mikhail Suslov and Leonid Brezhnev and the accession of Iurii Andropov. These events left unmistakable marks on the pages of *Nash sovremennik*.

How does one explain the journal's unusual boldness during these two years? First, there was the protection offered to the Russian nationalists in this period by ideological overseer Mikhail Suslov. This protection of Russian nationalists willing to work within the system to achieve their ends by

---

*This essay is a revised version of a paper presented at the Western Slavic Association Meetings, Hoover Institution, Stanford University, March 31, 1984.

the party secretary for ideology is, of course, a noteworthy development. Aware of the marked decline in the appeal of the official ideology to the populace, Suslov may have been investigating the possibility of a National Bolshevik orientation, in which a weakened and de-ideologized "Bolshevism" would be melded with a statist form of Russian nationalism.

Another factor behind the journal's boldness was the ominous – in the eyes of the nationalists – rise to power of elements that would eventually be able to unseat Brezhnev's chosen successor, Chernenko, and place Iurii Andropov at the party helm. It is difficult to find a label for them: essentially, they seem to have been an amalgam of technocrats, defense and heavy industry officials, and KGB representatives – believers in headlong modernization, the scientific and technical revolution, and the Soviet "melting pot." Expansionist in their external policies, they advocated running a tight political ship at home. For such elements, the Russian nationalists, with their outspoken preservationist views, their commitment to ethnic particularism (of non-Russians as well as Russians), and their flirtation with Orthodox Christianity represented an obscurantist group to be cudgeled into submission. Sensing the ascendancy of these elements, particularly after the invasion of Afghanistan in 1979, nationalist spokesmen such as Vladimir Soloukhin, Vadim Kozhinov, and Sergei Semanov issued warning salvos on the pages of *Nash sovremennik*.

That they were able to do so quasi-openly suggests that certain critical posts on the journal's editorial board during 1981–1982 must have been occupied by intrepid nationalists. And indeed, one notes that, beginning with the no. 2 (1981) issue, Iurii Seleznev and V. A. Ustinov became deputy editors to editor in chief Sergei Vikulov. In previous years, Seleznev, in particular, had shown himself to be a dedicated nationalist. (With the no. 10 [1981] issue, he became the journal's first deputy editor.)

Following the appointments of Seleznev and Ustinov, *Nash sovremennik* began to publish some extraordinary contributions. Thus the no. 3 (1981) issue carried a series of aphoristic reflections by Soloukhin entitled "Pebbles in the Palm [of a Hand]." In one of these "pebbles," Soloukhin unmistakably attempted to demonstrate the existence of God:

> In the twentieth century, for every healthy-minded man, there can be no doubt that there exists a rational principle (*razumnoe nachalo*) in the world, in the universe, in the diversity of life. . . . The question is not whether such a higher mind exists but whether it knows about me and has any concern for me.[36]

Unusual contents for a Soviet journal!

The no. 6 issue of the journal for 1981 added something nearly as striking. On the inside front cover, there unexpectedly appeared the motto "*Rossiia – rodina moia*" (Russia – my homeland), under which was placed the first of what were to be many pictures epitomizing the motherland. In the no. 6 issue, a copse of Russian birch trees was chosen. Within the Soviet political context, this clear-cut invocation of Russia – as opposed to the supraethnic USSR – in a journal of the RSFSR Union of Writers had important overtones. In subsequent issues, the reader was offered varied images of Russia – decorative peasant huts, winding country lanes, peasant lads in army uniform; on occasion, Lenin found his way into the pictures, but always in a subsidiary role.

The year 1981 marked the 100th anniversary of Dostoevskii's death, and *Nash sovremennik* made use of this hallowed anniversary to make what it regarded as necessary political points. Especially noteworthy was a piece by Vadim Kozhinov in the no. 11 issue for 1981.[37] In this controversial essay, Kozhinov developed certain ideas formulated by the Eurasians and by Soviet scholar Lev Gumilev and dwelled on the significance of the Battle of Kulikovo Field, the 600th anniversary of which was celebrated in 1980. Like the Dostoevskii anniversary, the remembrance of Kulikovo Field has great symbolic importance for the nationalists. In his article, Kozhinov offers a peroration on the great fourteenth-century battle, which he sees, oddly, as a decisive struggle between the "multinational Russian state" and an "aggressive cosmopolitan armada" representing the "dark forces" of the world at that time.[38] Kozhinov's barbs were not directed at the Tatar-Mongols but at the Andropovites, who were beginning to make a serious bid for power. (In a few months' time, the Andropovites would pay him back in kind, and with interest.)

A similar attack on the Andropov coalition had been made by nationalist tribune Sergei Semanov in a book review published in the no. 7 (1981) issue.[39] Reviewing a book on Trotskyism brought out by *Molodaia gvardiia* publishing house in 1979, he wrote:

> Trotskii openly declared himself an adherent of "revolutionary aggressiveness" and demanded that the country of the victorious proletariat should carry the revolution on "red bayonets" to other countries. More than once, Trotskii tried to support his belief in a "revolutionary war" between Soviet Russia and international capitalism with practical actions. Thus in 1919, he recommended that 30–40,000 horsemen be sent to India. . . .

Here was a scarcely-veiled denunciation of the invasion of Afghanistan and of Soviet military adventures abroad.

Elsewhere, Semanov fulminated against the alleged "elitism" of Trotskyites past and present:

> A Trotskyite elite of "the chosen" is to rule society supposedly in the name of the people. As for the popular masses, they are "ants of the revolution," as L. D. Trotskii (Bronshtein) himself put it. The lot of the masses is to live within the confines of a barracks society and be obedient.

The regime of Hafizullah Amin in Afghanistan, which "'abolished' religion, destroyed the clergy, and defiled mosques" in a country where 90 percent of the populace was Muslim is cited as an instance of modern-day Trotskyism, as are the Khmer Rouge in Cambodia who "sliced up more than 3 million inhabitants in their country while creating a 'new society.'"

Semanov clearly had "Trotskyites" nearer home in mind as well. For him the Andropovites constitute an amalgam of Jews and denationalized Russians who advocate a path that is suicidal for Russia, a country that has already paid a terrible price for the fanaticism of the 1920s and 1930s. The invasion of Afghanistan is seen as the first step in a process of Russian national self-destruction. (The Andropovites would remember Semanov, too, in the months to come.)

During 1981–1982 *Nash sovremennik* also focused on issues with which one might expect a Russian nationalist publication to be concerned: the preservation of the environment and of Russian historical monuments,[40] the preservation of ethnic Russians themselves from the scourge of alcoholism and the breakup of the family,[41] and the need to recover the vivifying mind and mores of traditional peasant Russia.[42] (In this regard, there was also a fascinating series by ruralist writer Vasilii Belov, entitled "Lad" (Concord), in which an ABCs of peasant customs and traditions – including the rite of baptism – are included.)[43]

Toward the end of 1981 and the beginning of 1982, the stridency of *Nash sovremennik* became especially noticeable. By this time, Andropov and his associates were already openly making aggressive moves on Brezhnev and his family (e.g., the so-called Gypsy affair, in which Brezhnev's daughter was implicated in a smuggling ring, and a thinly veiled attack on Brezhnev in the journal *Avrora*[44]). In the no. 1 (1982) issue of *Nash sovremennik*, Soloukhin assailed the destruction of Russian historical monuments with unusual vehemence and sharply criticized the turning of ancient churches into museums of atheism and planetaria.[45] Among the editors and contributors to the journal there seems to have been a sense of time running out.

On January 19, 1982, the nationalists' all-powerful protector, Mikhail Suslov, died. The journal's opponents moved immediately and decisively to exploit this event.

Only days after Suslov's death, the no. 2 (1982) issue of

Kommunist went to press containing two sharp attacks on Soloukhin for his alleged "flirtation with dear little god".[46] (Although Soloukhin had been criticized in the journals *Nauka i religiia* and *Znamia* during 1981, Suslov's protection had saved him from undue unpleasantness.[47]) Soloukhin's attempt to demonstrate the existence of God in the no. 3 (1981) issue of *Nash sovremennik* was the focal point of the *Kommunist* attack.

Several days later, *Pravda* came out with an equally severe assault on Vadim Kozhinov, Iurii Seleznev, and other interpreters of Dostoevskii for flagrantly failing to adhere to Marxist-Leninist aesthetic criteria.[48] The singling out of the first deputy editor of *Nash sovremennik*, Seleznev, was a noteworthy development. Through cannonades in the infallible *Kommunist* and magisterial *Pravda*, the Andropovites were serving notice to the nationalists that they had better submit or be destroyed.

During February, March, and April of 1982, a fascinating, albeit brutal, struggle took place, one reflected on the pages of *Nash sovremennik*. On February 18, the no. 3 (1982) issue of the journal went to press conspicuously shorn of its motto "Russia – my homeland," but containing a continuation of Soloukhin's "Pebbles in the Palm," a work that had just been excoriated by *Kommunist*. Moreover, in one of the "pebbles," Soloukhin once again undertook to demonstrate the existence of God.[49] One wonders whether *Kommunist* had ever been previously so challenged.

The no. 4 (1982) number of *Nash sovremennik*, which went to press on March 19, once again carried the motto "Russia – my homeland." By this time, however, the journal's adversaries had apparently resolved on a purge.

The purge seems to have occurred in April. On the 27th of that month, the no. 5 issue went to press with a dramatically altered editorial board. Gone was First Deputy Editor Seleznev. Removed as deputy editor was V. A. Ustinov. And *five* new members were now added: S. I. Zhuravlev, V. I. Korobov, A. G. Kuz'min, A. F. Shitikov, and N. E. Shundik. One of the new editors, Kuz'min, had sharply attacked Vadim Kozhinov in the previous issue of the journal.[50] The following month, May – the month in which Andropov officially moved over to the Secretariat and assumed the mantle of secretary for ideology – *Kommunist* cleaned up on some unfinished business. On May 19, the no. 8 issue of *Kommunist* went to press containing apologies from Editor in Chief Vikulov and the party committee of *Nash sovremennik* for Soloukhin's offending piece in the journal's 1981, no. 3 issue.[51] Soloukhin was quoted, secondhand, as apologizing for what he had written and as asserting that he was and had always been an atheist. Thus it took *Kommunist* four months to extract not precisely groveling apologies from the nationalists gathered around *Nash sovremennik*.

The remaining issues of *Nash sovremennik* for 1982 – numbers 6 to 12 – are notably less bold than those of the previous 18 months; still, they cannot be described as altogether bland. In this period, one perceives a journal that is bowed but not broken.

In November 1982, the death of General Secretary Brezhnev occurred, an event that inevitably affected the fortunes of the nationalists. Although it permitted Andropov to emerge as general secretary, it also required him to surrender the crucial ideological portfolio to his rival, Chernenko, who appeared to be more cautious in his approach to the nationalists than Andropov.

The no. 12 issue of *Nash sovremennik* for 1982, which went to press on December 1, reflects the beginning of this transaction. The inside cover is once again blank – no "Russia – my homeland" – but the issue contains warm and effusive praise for the late general secretary and only a tepid acknowledgment of the new one, Iurii Andropov.

The study of *Nash sovremennik* for 1981 and 1982 casts useful light on a number of questions. It demonstrates the considerable strength of the Russian nationalist tendency (to the point where it enjoyed the protection of the second party secretary) and also points up its many vulnerabilities. An important debate – as well as a brutal political struggle – has been taking place in the USSR over such issues as modernization, Westernization, military expansion, and the Soviet melting pot, a debate reflected on the pages of *Nash sovremennik*.

3

The Fortunes of Russian Nationalists under Chernenko

When Konstantin Chernenko became general secretary following the death of Iurii Andropov in early 1984, one was justifiably uncertain as to what policy his regime would follow via-à-vis the Russian party. Would Chernenko and his associates seek to emulate Brezhnev and Suslov and achieve a cautious modus vivendi with the Russian nationalists, or would they continue Andropov's overtly hostile line, attempting to reduce the nationalists' power and influence? At first it appeared that a policy roughly similar to that of Andropov was being followed. My Hoover Institution colleague Mikhail Bernstam has suggested this explanation for the Chernenko regime's early stance toward the Russian nationalists:

> The most consistent domestic policy of the Chernenko administration has been a vigorous attempt to create a uniform communist society. If one assumes that such a monolithic society, with no or minimal centripetal forces, had already existed under Stalin but dispersed thereafter, then Chernenko's policy amounts to a restoration. At any rate, this is a new and ambitious social policy, and a major reversal of the last 30 years.
>
> In order to implement such a policy, the Chernenko administration has to bring the entire social and cultural life of the country into uniformity, to crush any

> possible type of semiofficial and nonofficial dissent, to eliminate all potential centripetal movements and to contain all, even slightly independent, individual or group expressions of opinion different from those of the leadership. The three major targets of this offensive were 1) representatives of conservative Russian nationalism, 2) the liberal dissidents, as well as potential reformers within the establishment, and 3) the non-Russian minorities [particularly the Uzbeks and Estonians] and their political elite.[52]

The month of May 1984 produced two significant indicators that the Chernenko regime was seeking to continue, and perhaps stiffen, Andropov's harsh line toward the Russian nationalists. On the sixth of the month, *Pravda* published a decree by the Party Central Committee and the Council of Ministers, one of whose clear purposes was to combat the Russian nationalist tendency in Soviet film.[53] As *The Times* of London reported, the decree was in part directed at the "nostalgia for the tsarist era which permeates recent films like *Anna Pavlova*" as well as at "films praising timeless rural values."[54] The decree fulminates against "dismal descriptions of mores (*bytopisatel'stvo*)" and the idealization of "obsolete moral norms and bases of life," unmistakable references to films inspired by nationalist sentiment. What Chernenko and the ideological apparatus appeared to want, *The Times* suggested, was a return to the "milk maid meets collective farm driver" brand of socialist realism that characterized the Stalin era. The newspaper also noted that one of the senior executives of Goskino, the state cinema organization, is Vladimir Chernenko, the son of the general secretary.[55]

On the twenty-first of the month, *Pravda* carried a prominently displayed book review by V. Oskotskii entitled "In the Struggle with Anti-Historicism."[56] The title of the article may have been intended to echo that of one of the severest attacks made against the nationalists during the Brezhnev period: Aleksandr Iakovlev's "Against Anti-Historicism," which was published in *Literaturnaia gazeta* in 1972 and served to raise nationalist hackles as few attacks before it.[57]

(As a result of this article, Iakovlev, the acting head of the Central Committee Department of Agitation and Propaganda, was "exiled" to Ottawa as ambassador, whence he was returned a decade later by Andropov to be made director of the Institute of World Economics and International Relations [IMEMO]. Iakovlev's summons home was a clear indication that the nationalists were in trouble.)

Oskotskii's review, which is of S. T. Kaltakhchian's *The Marxist-Leninist Theory of the Nation and Contemporaneity*,[58] is primarily intended as a diatribe against the Russian nationalists. Oskotskii lashes out against the "single stream" theory of national historical development favored by the nationalists and sharply criticizes "antiscientific attempts to deny the immutable actuality of the Leninist criteria of 'two nations' and 'two cultures'. . . ." For Oskotskii, as for Lenin, the year 1917 represents a decisive break with prerevolutionary historical development and a leap into a higher, sacred reality. There is no unbroken historical continuum, no single stream.

> Under the guise of a repudiation of vulgar sociologism, some scholars repudiate sociologism in general and articulate a conciliatory attitude toward the ideology of pan-Slavism, as well as the reactionary positions of the ideology of "liberal renegadism" and of direct apologists for autocracy. There are also statements about religious activists, about *startsy* [elders], who supposedly express the spirit of the nation, and about religion as the fount of elevated morality. . . . In some publications, the national character is "extracted" from the non-class, absolute morality of a "national spirit," and peasant patriarchal-ness is seen as a primal source for everything national.

Through Oskotskii's doctrinnaire prose, we become acquainted with at least some of the reasons for the Chernenko regime's unhappiness with the nationalists. Pan-Slavism, the ideas of the 1909 *Vekhi* collection (christened "liberal renegadism" by Lenin), and monarchism are seen as directly incompatible with the regime's legitimizing ideology. Equally as odious are writings, such as those by nationalist tribune Vladimir Soloukhin, which extol the *startsy* and Russian Orthodox Christianity as emanations of the national spirit, while the exaltation of the traditional patriarchal peasant village by the *derevenshchiki* (i.e., by such writers as Valentin Rasputin, Vasilii Belov, and the late Fedor Abramov) stands athwart the Soviet Union's commitment to rapid modernization.

Oskotskii's shrillness and his failure, at least pro forma, to balance his criticism of the Russian party with cautions directed at "bourgeois nationalists" (i.e., nationalists among the minority peoples of the USSR) indicates the extent of the regime's unhappiness with and concern over the Russian nationalists. As for the book *The Marxist-Leninist Theory of the Nation and Contemporaneity*, it represents an unsparing attack on the Russian nationalists by an Armenian author. The book's author, S. T. Kaltakhchian, repeatedly cites Andropov's writings on the nationalities issue and seeks to portray himself as a disciple of the late general secretary on this important question. In his study, Kaltakhchian singles out a number of Russian nationalists (significantly, only Russian nationalists) for opprobrium: Mikhail Lobanov, Vadim Kozhinov, Lev Gumilev, Valentin Rasputin, and others. Concerning Lobanov, for example, he writes: "M. Lobanov, ignoring the just critical comments which have repeatedly been directed at him, published an article entitled 'liberation' in the October 1982 issue of *Volga* in which, from a position of antihistoricism, he continues to insist on his former mistaken reasonings concerning 'the heavy cross of national self-awareness' and 'the call of natural wholeness.'"[59] The implied threat to Lobanov is clear.

Kaltakhchian likewise assails "neo-*pochvennik* motifs" in the writings of Soviet authors (the reference is, of course, to the nineteenth century *pochvenniki*, i.e., such writers as Dostoevskii and Apollon Grigor'ev) and attacks "the apology for peasant patriarchal-ness" contained in the works of the *derevenshchiki*.[60] He also criticizes those who attempt to distort the writings of Tolstoi and Dostoevskii for their own purposes,[61] and he ominously labels "anti-Communist" those nationalists who seek to oppose the "scientific and technical revolution."[62] Referring to Valentin Rasputin's controversial nationalist novel, *Farewell to Matera*, Kaltakhchian stresses that even Rasputin believes "it is already impossible to return to Matera," that is, to traditional, patriarchal Russia.[63]

As against the antihistorical and anti-Communist ideas of the Russian nationalists, Kaltakhchian elaborates a "scientific" theory concerning the gradual emergence of Soviet man. Significantly, two of the chapters of his book are entitled "The Formation of the One Culture of the Soviet People" and "The Development of the Culture of the One Soviet People," suggesting that the constituent peoples of the USSR are gradually merging together into an entity called "the Soviet people" (*sovetskii narod*), a conception that is of course anathema to the Russian party.

The fact that Kaltakhchian, an ethnic Armenian, felt free to cudgel the Russian nationalists without directing compensatory blows at the minority nationalists shows the extent to which the Andropov leadership was tilting against the Russian party. By putting its imprimatur on this quite extreme book, Chernenko's *Pravda* took a radical stance that would have been unusual under Brezhnev and Suslov. In unambiguously terming the nationalists anti-Communists, Kaltakhchian would seem to be calling for a purge.

At approximately the same time as the Russian nationalists were being vilified in *Pravda*, perhaps the most startling development of the Chernenko period was being prepared: the "rehabilitation" of nationalist tribune Vladimir Soloukhin. In June 1984, Soloukhin was awarded the prestigious Order of the Red Banner of Labor by the Supreme Soviet of the USSR for "his services in the development of Soviet literature and in connection with his 60th birthday.[64] Only a year previously Soloukhin had been harshly criticized on the pages of *Kommunist*. As if this were not enough, other Russian party writers who had been out of favor under Andropov were likewise singled out for awards: Viktor Astaf'ev, Iurii Bondarev, Leonid Leonov. Nationalist writer Mikhail Alekseev's important anticollectivization novel, *Drachuny* (Pugnacious

Fellows, 1981), was permitted to be nominated for a Lenin prize, though it did not in fact receive the award.[65] Obviously a major comeback had been achieved by the nationalists.

Mikhail Bernstam has offered the following explanation for the nationalists' resurgence:

> . . . . in the Summer of 1984, the Chernenko administration had to retreat in its policy towards this group [i.e., the Russian nationalist writers]. Soloukhin, Astaf'ev, and other nationalist authors have been decorated with high state orders and awards. This was a major embarrassment and the most significant setback for Chernenko's policies since his assumption of power. The recent Party campaigns and ideological decisions which were the cornerstones of Chernenko's course had to be ignored and even tacitly reversed in respect to a small group of independent intellectuals.
>
> A new social force, alone among many under attack, appeared to possess a certain unexpected influence against which the Soviet leadership was compelled to retreat. The explanation probably lies in the fact that the leadership is aware that the small group of Russian nationalist writers has a strong social appeal to millions of citizens among ethnic Russians. . . . [66]

An address by Chernenko to a plenum of the Soviet Writers' Union, held in late September 1984, offers additional evidence that a tactical retreat is under way. As Radio Liberty analyst Sergei Yurenen has pointed out, there are striking differences in tone and content between this address and Chernenko's "benchmark" speech on ideological issues in June 1983. In the 1984 address, the attitude toward the National Bolsheviks is, in Yurenen's words, "one of encouragement."[67] Absent are the antinationalist and antireligious sentiments that characterized the earlier 1983 address. Unlike Yurenen, I would not ascribe this change to Chernenko's having to reflect Andropov's views in the 1983 speech. During his first months as general secretary, Chernenko showed himself to be as principled an antinationalist as Andropov. What seems to have happened, rather, is a retreat by Chernenko before a determined counteroffensive by the Russian nationalists.

Even more compelling evidence of the nationalists' resurgence is the list of prizes given to Soviet writers "for services in the development of Soviet literature and in connection with the fiftieth anniversary of the formation of the Union of Writers of the USSR," which was published in late November 1984 in *Literaturnaia gazeta*.[68] Five militant nationalist spokesmen – Vasilii Belov, Egor Isaev, Evgenii Nosov, Petr Proskurin, and Valentin Rasputin – were awarded the exceptionally prestigious Order of Lenin, and a number of other nationalist writers received lesser commendations. The dark days of the Andropov persecution had seemingly come to an end.

In originally choosing an anti-Russian nationalist orientation, the Chernenko regime, like the Andropov leadership before it, took a politically risky step, one from which it apparently decided to make a tactical retreat. Alain Besançon has provided a useful explanation of the regime's dilemma. Writing in early 1983 concerning possible future Soviet policies on the nationalities question, he reflected:

> From the Bolshevik point of view, there are only two possible policies. The first would be a return to strict Leninism, which is what Stalin dreamed of accomplishing in his last years. This policy would entail the destruction of the nationalities, which would be mixed together in the magma of Sovietism, with a Russian flavor, no doubt – but where even the Russian nation would lose its strength. It appears as if the current [Andropov] regime does not have the strength to try such a policy. . . .

And he continued:

> The second policy would be to increase the privileges and extend further the Russian-Bolshevik alliance by abandoning the compromises reached with the non-Russian nationalities. The practical effect of this step would be to restore officially the Russian empire and

> abandon the fiction of a Soviet Union. . . . Although this change of course toward a "national Bolshevism" might be tempting, *and much as the natural evolution of the Soviet world seems to point in that direction*, it runs aground ineluctably on the question of the legitimacy of power. . . . (Italics added.)

Besançon then concludes that the only logical path for the regime to take is to "sight-navigate between an impossible return to Stalinism and the dangerous currents of National Bolshevism."[69]

As always, Besançon's comments are both incisive and provocative; yet what actually happened under Andropov and, at first, under Chernenko directly contradicted his sensible prophecy. Both the Andropov and Chernenko regimes did choose to return to a policy of strict Leninism on the nationalities issue. Indeed they went further than Stalin in his last years; the "Russian flavor" (with the exception of the Russian language, which has to serve as the *lingua franca* of the Soviet state) of the "magma of Sovietism" appeared to be a matter of indifference to them. The revolutionary implications of such a development are not difficult to discern. By heavy-handedly opting for a policy of strict Leninism on the nationalities issue, the Andropov and Chernenko leaderships galvanized and radicalized nationally minded ethnic Russians. The hasty retreat by the Chernenko leadership in mid-1984 may presage other concessions to the Russian nationalists in the near future.

Postscript

The death of Konstantin Chernenko in March 1985 and the accession of Mikhail Gorbachev have undoubtedly affected the fortunes of Russian nationalists in important ways, but it is too early to say precisely how. It is probably a tribute to Gorbachev's formidable political skills that his beliefs and sentiments concerning the nationalists remain screened from foreign observers; as the Politburo "heir apparent," it would have been risky for him to exhibit too definite a profile on such a controversial issue.

Certain shreds of evidence suggest that Gorbachev may have some sympathy for the nationalists and their causes. The marked improvement in the position of Russian nationalist writers during the second half of Chernenko's brief reign coincided with Gorbachev's occupying the post of party secretary for ideology. Chernenko, however, often trespassed upon the younger man's turf in this sphere, and one simply does not know to what extent the amelioration of the nationalists' position was due to Gorbachev's influence and to what extent to other factors.

Writing in the September 23, 1984 issue of the *Washington Post*, Robert Kaiser reported "persistent rumors from credible (Soviet) academic sources" that Gorbachev had asked economists for briefings on the agrarian reforms of Petr Stolypin, Nicholas II's prime minister, and on Lenin's New Economic Policy (NEP). Stolypin's reform and the NEP – both of which admitted significant market forces into the economy – are popular with Russian nationalist intellectuals, while the figure of Stolypin himself is sacrosanct to Aleksandr Solzhenitsyn, among others. In this case, too, however, the evidence concerning Gorbachev's views is flimsy.

Contrary evidence can also be adduced that Gorbachev is in fact hostile to the nationalists and their causes. For example, Western observers have frequently noted that he has sought to identify himself with Andropov and his legacy of economic reform. In light of the fact that Andropov was a fierce opponent of the nationalists, one wonders whether Gorbachev would do this if he were a strong nationalist sympathizer.

One other aspect of the Gorbachev accession deserves some comment. Certain Western analysts believe that they have perceived signs that the Soviet military is less than enthusiastic about Gorbachev's ascendancy. Were this unhappiness to intensify, the military might be tempted to back a rival Politburo candidate, and Gorbachev's tenure, like

Georgii Malenkov's before him, could turn out to be quite short. Russian nationalist sentiment in the military is said to be strong.

As of late April 1985, Gorbachev's views concerning the nationalists and their causes were not clearly discernible.

4

Russian Nationalism, the West, and the Problem of Soviet Jews

Marxism-Leninism serves as the legitimizing ideology of the USSR and as the driving force behind Soviet expansion abroad. It is also the glue that holds the Soviet "empire" together; without this glue, the nations of Eastern Europe could not be held, and it is doubtful whether, in the absence of significant concessions, many of the minority republics of the Soviet Union could be retained. As Alain Besançon has aptly put it: ". . . . power in the USSR is the pendant of ideology, which is the legitimizing support for it, and if the ideology were withdrawn, power would crumble."[70]

Fortunately for the West, Marxist-Leninist ideology has lost its hold over the Soviet populace. It has entirely lost its élan and can no longer serve to inspire, motivate, or mobilize the Soviet citizenry. Vladimir Voinovich's comment is typical of independent observers: ". . . . ideology, communist ideology, lies in ruins. . . . I, for one, do not know a single person in the Soviet Union who believes in it."[71] The published results of Soviet polls likewise point to a dramatic decline in the appeal of the official ideology.[72] Marxism-Leninism is a "dead" ideology, and its demise as a living force has created a vacuum that must inevitably be filled by other ideologies and belief systems.

Despite the fact that Marxism-Leninism is dead, the

present Soviet leadership needs it more than ever. As Alexander Shtromas has noted:

> They [the Soviet rulers] could not do without it, since they are not representative of anybody or anything except this "ultimate" ideology. . . . There is probably even more real substance in the Soviet rulership's commitment to Communist world domination at present than there was at any other time. For now it is not any more only abstract ideals but the plain survival of a ruthless and cynical power-clique which is at stake. . . . In order to keep its people in submission, the Soviet state has to impress them constantly and convincingly with its irresistible might. Expansion serves this purpose best.[73]

The death of the Soviet Union's legitimizing ideology presents the West with perhaps its best opportunity in decades to help bring the expansionist Soviet juggernaut to a halt and thereby save Western taxpayers billions of dollars in armament outlays (as well as rescuing future Third World countries from falling victim to the "Communist experiment"). The contemporary West has a unique chance to serve as a "midwife of history" and assist a new political reality struggling to be born. So important is this development that it is now theoretically possible to speak not merely of "containing" the Soviet Union, or of "rolling back" its achievements, but of "victory" (in the sense of terminating Marxism-Leninism's stranglehold on the USSR and the countries of Eastern Europe).

The instrument by which the West can most effectively serve as a midwife of history is the foreign radio – Radio Liberty, the Voice of America, BBC, Deutsche Welle, for example – which is listened to by some 60 million Soviet citizens[74] and whose immense influence Soviet jamming has been unable to curtail. Indeed one is told by specialists that, with a modest infusion of funds, the technology of broadcasting should be able to stay ahead of that of jamming, a process that, incidentally, is considerably more expensive than broadcasting. (The publication of Russian language books in the West represents a second vehicle for reaching the Soviet citizenry; such books more or less automatically achieve circulation in the USSR once they appear in *tamizdat.*)

Of the various ideologies and belief systems moving in to fill the vacuum created by the death of Marxist ideology, one is of particular importance: Russian nationalism. Because of the position of its supporters and sympathizers in various Soviet elites, it has the most realistic chance to succeed Marxism-Leninism as the ruling ideology of the Soviet Union. In fact, its advent may be historically preconditioned, as it is currently being pushed to the fore by the natural evolution of the Russian Revolution. The triumph of Russian nationalism would usher in a political system markedly different from the current one. As Besançon writes: "There would be significant and immediate advantages to making official the pan-Russian Military and Police Empire: all those advantages that would flow from the suppression of ideology. This would be an enormous relief to the regime's subjects."[75] Note that Besançon refers to all the regime's subjects, not simply to ethnic Russians. By relaxing the present Soviet regime's ideocratic grip on the country, a Russian nationalist government would permit the constituent peoples of the USSR to begin to breathe. Indeed, a Russian nationalist government would have to come to an understanding with the minority peoples of the USSR, granting them, as a minimum, broad autonomy; in the absence of such understanding, the present-day USSR would inevitably disintegrate.

"There is no doubt," write Victor Zaslavskii and Robert Brym in their recent study, *Soviet-Jewish Emigration and Soviet Nationality Policy*, "that Russian nationalism . . . has, on the whole, an anti-Soviet character."[76] Alexander Shtromas makes the same point: "One should not forget that Russian nationalism has always been and still is essentially anti-Communist and as such, should be considered as a force basically opposed to the Soviet political regime. . . . "[77] The ideology of Marxism-Leninism is increasingly seen by contemporary Russian nationalists as incompatible with the vital interests, indeed the survival, of the ethnic Russian people. Marxism-Leninism and Russian nationalism now find themselves on the opposite side of the barricades on most of the issues that command the attention of current Russian nationalists: the preservation of ethnic Russians themselves from sociodemographic attrition (plummeting birth rates, alcoholism, juvenile deliquency, etc.); the safeguarding of ancient Russian historical monuments and of the natural environment; the preservation of the national religion, Russian Orthodoxy, from extinction; the rescuing of the Russian language from bastardization resulting from its use as the "language of ideology"; the resurrection of the thought of nationalist thinkers of the past, such as Dostoevskii and Aleksei Khomiakov. There seems to be no way, today, that such fervent concerns can be melded with the official ideology, and the alienation of Russian nationalists therefore continues apace. Realizing this, the Andropov regime abandoned any attempts at accommodation with Russian nationalism and instead sought to effect its diminution as a political force. The Chernenko regime appears originally to have emulated Andropov's approach, then to have performed a tactical retreat from it.

Given the above situation, what is the contemporary West to do? The West would seem to have three options before it: it may elect to be neutral in the emerging struggle between a dying regime (one, it should be stressed, that is committed to undermining the West politically) and its Russian nationalist adversaries; it may choose to serve as "a midwife of history," largely through its broadcasting policies toward ethnic Russians in the Soviet Union; or it may attempt to use its resources to prevent the Russian nationalists from coming to power and thereby to prolong the existence of the present Marxist-Leninist regime. Strange as it may appear, there exist scholars and diplomats in the West who seriously contemplate advocating the last policy. They even have a spokesman: recent émigré Alexander Yanov, who urges a Western effort on the scale of the Marshall Plan to ensure that the nationalists do not come to power.[78]

Two worrisome traits of the Russian nationalists tempt Western policymakers to contemplate adopting such a course. First, there are the perceived authoritarian proclivities of many nationalists, especially those in the military.[79] Concerning this problem, one should state the obvious: it is clear that the next government of the USSR is not likely to be polyarchic in the Western sense. There has simply been no preparation for the emergence of a U.S.-style democracy; in politics, one seldom witnesses a creation *ex nihilo*. On the other hand, a Franco-type government (which could be in the wings) might eventually prepare the way for democracy, as happened in post-Franco Spain. Authoritarianism is not totalitarianism. Chalmers Johnson defines totalitarianism thus: "The concentration of all power and all authority in the hands of the government would be an ideal definition of totalitarianism."[80] It would also be a good definition of the Andropov and Chernenko regimes.

For the West to allow the problem of authoritarianism to stand in the way of its taking at least a neutral stand toward the Russian nationalists strikes one as foolhardy. The termination of Marxism-Leninism's hegemony in the Soviet Union would be of immediate and immense benefit to the West and indeed to all countries of the world. As Crane Brinton noted decades ago, there is a critical difference between a Russia acting as a conventional world power and a Russia "expanding as the Arabs expanded, in the name of a fierce and intolerant faith."[81]

The Problem of Soviet Jews

There can be little doubt that anti-Semitism, including a belief in an alleged "Jewish-Masonic conspiracy," is a major current in the ranks of contemporary Russian nationalists. This fact understandably induces Jews both in the USSR and abroad to contemplate an all-out campaign against this current. Indeed Yanov, a Soviet Jewish émigré, has already launched one. Although there are Soviet Jews who feel quite differently about Russian nationalism – Shtromas, for example, a 1973 émigré, a Lithuanian Jew, and the survivor of a Nazi concentration camp – it is likely that a majority of thinking Jews find the Russian nationalist tendency worrisome. One might add that the issue of Russian nationalist-Soviet Jewish relations inevitably expands to involve Western governments, which are subject to the influence of Jewish lobbies and which are consequently seen by many Russian nationalists as in thrall to an omnipotent Jewish conspiracy. It is surely the "Jewish question" that most threatens future good relations between the West and a Russian nationalist government.

Without being fatuous, a constructive dialogue between Russian nationalists and Jews does seem possible. Indeed, such a dialogue occurred in the early 1970s between Zionist activist Mikhail Agurskii, before his emigration to Israel, and the editors of the nationalist *samizdat* journal *Veche*.[82] It should not be forgotten that Russians and Jews share a frightful bond: both have been the victims, in this century, of monstrous holocausts. Stalin's holocaust took some 20 million lives, while the war against Nazi Germany took another 20 million (a majority of the victims of both these plagues being ethnic Russians); Hitler's carnage of the Jews is well known. In light of their grisly experiences, Russians and Jews are understandably concerned, even obsessed, with the question of national survival. Confronted with deleterious demographic and social trends, some contemporary ethnic Russians wonder whether their people will continue to be able to play a significant role in history. As Agurskii has put it: ". . . . Jews often perceive the Russian national movement as aggressive, whereas in essence it is a defensive one."[83] The same, of course, holds true for the Jewish "national movement," which sees itself continually under threat from unwelcome social and demographic developments such as the birth rate of Israeli Arabs, Khomeiniism, social strains, and economic dislocations at home.

Relations between Russian nationalists and Soviet Jews must be considered in their historical and social context. To take the historical context first, both Russians and Jews have justification for mutual resentment. Jews unjustly suffered second-class citizenship following Russia's annexation of Poland in the late eighteenth century (there were no Jews to speak of in Russia before then), and, after 1881, they were the victims of pogroms that were incited by extremist Russian nationalists (and condemned by moderate nationalists and Russian churchmen). In addition, Stalin's savage campaign, in the last years of his reign, against "rootless cosmopolitans" was cynically abetted by more than a few ethnic Russians.

As for Russians, they suffered at the hands of Soviet Jews from 1917 to 1934, when Jews were deemed "the most reliable element" in the Soviet Union and moved in to fill the decimated ranks of a politically suspect ethnic Russian intelligentsia. A number of the first Bolshevik leaders were Jews, as were some high-ranking secret police officials and concentration camp chiefs. Iakov Iurovskii, the man who shot Emperor Nicholas II and his son, the *Tsarevich* Alexis, appears to have been a Jew. Jews, as Agurskii points out, were heavily involved in the harsh persecution of the Russian Orthodox Church, while the persecution of religious Jews was left to Communist Jews.[84] It is essential to stress here that these Jews thought of themselves as Communists, not Jews; they were often extremely hostile to their Jewish heritage. Contemplating this dismal history, one concludes that the "mutual forgiveness of nations" advocated by Solzhenitsyn and his cocontributors to the collection *From Under the Rubble* may in fact be the only pragmatic solution to the mutual animosities of Russians and Soviet Jews.

The social context of this problem is equally important. As Victor Zaslavskii (a Soviet Jewish émigré) and Robert Brym point out in their recent study, much of the tension between contemporary Jews and Russians in the USSR is social and structural.[85] Although certain professions in the Soviet Union have gradually eliminated all Jews, especially the military officer corps and the foreign service, Jews have nonetheless been able to achieve remarkable success in other professions. The extraordinary over-representation of Jews—who constitute only 1 percent of the Soviet populace—in such professions as science, mathematics, law, and medicine now leads to cries for "affirmative action" on the part of ethnic Russians—who constitute 52 percent of the populace—and of minority nationalities who covet the positions currently held by Soviet Jews.

Tensions between Russians and Jews are especially exacerbated in the literary and artistic fields. As Zaslavskii and Brym write: "It is anything but accidental that anti-Jewish sentiments are especially strong within the so-called creative literary and artistic intelligentsia, for this group embodies the quintessence of the national spirit yet also has a high concentration of completely Russified Jews."[86] One frequently hears Russian nationalists complain, for example, that Jews make up a majority of the influential Moscow chapter of the Writers' Union.

At this juncture, it might be useful to introduce a distinction made by Zaslavskii and Brym between "periphery" Jews (i.e., those in the Baltic, Georgia, and other borderland areas) and "heartland" Jews (i.e., those in the RSFSR and the Ukraine). The latter tend to be the most assimilated within the USSR and the least committed to Judaism as a religion. When they are able to emigrate, close to 90 percent choose to go to North America or Western Europe rather than to Israel. Zionism is weakly represented among heartland Jews, while it is quite strong among Jews in the periphery. It should be stressed that it is the heartland Jews who must inevitably clash with the Russian nationalists. Zaslavskii and Brym explain why: ". . . . the structural position of the Jews in Soviet society determines the fact that the ideas of internationalism and universalism, even if presented in the quite particular form of Sovietization, continue to have an irresistible appeal to the Jewish intelligentsia."[87] Such Jews were natural allies for the nationalities' policies of the Andropov regime and natural opponents for the Russian nationalists, who vehemently oppose a merging of Soviet peoples into a denationalized "Soviet man" or "Soviet people" (*narod*).

A careful reading of the writings of contemporary Russian nationalists, as well as conversations with representatives of this tendency in the so-called third emigration, lead one to conclude that most Russian nationalists countenance two solutions to the "Jewish problem": the emigration of all Jews abroad (Zionists to Israel and heartlanders to North America and Western Europe) or the establishment of a Jewish republic, perhaps to be located in the Crimea (and not, like the infamous Birobidzhan, in Siberia), on the model of the other national republics. Such solutions, which would involve uprooting close to 2 million people, can hardly find favor among the citizens of a democracy such as the United States; they are, however, clearly preferable to other worst case scenarios. As recent émigré Simon Markish has written in *Soviet Jewish Affairs*:

> Liberalization, democratization, humanization of the regime in the spirit of Sakharov or Medvedev would most likely bring some benefit to the Jews; but the likelihood of the "Democrats" succeeding is negligible. . . . Another scenario for the future – the nationalistic – is more feasible. Such a policy commands considerably greater sympathy among the oppressed population, even among the oppressing New Class. At worst, it would be a form of Russian Hitlerism, and at best, the incarnation of Solzhenitsyn's ideals. Of the former case, nothing is to be said, it is quite clear; as for the latter case, the Jews would at least acquire the right of unobstructed emigration and religious freedom. But no more. . . . Solzhenitsyn does not wish us evil, he genuinely wishes us good – in our own house, in our own affairs, in our own land. For nationally-conscious Jews this is all that is necessary; for the assimilationists, it is a warning not to fall into the trap yet again.[88]

As Agurskii, Markish, and others point out, the proposed Russian nationalist solutions present no threat to Zionists or religious Jews in the Soviet Union; freedom to emigrate and to practice their religion is all that they desire. Such solutions do, however, bode ill for assimilationist heartland Jews who desire to maintain their hard-earned middle class positions and privileges (positions and privileges which, however, as Zaslavskii and Brym show, are being gradually eroded). The problem for the Israeli government and for Jews in the diaspora, as well as for Western governments, would seem to be whether to acquiesce to the solutions – that is, emigration or a Jewish republic – offered by the Russian nationalists or to launch an all-out campaign to mobilize Western public opinion against them. The danger, of course, is that such a campaign could backfire.

Before concluding this section, one should briefly note the existence of other ethnic lobbies that likewise have influenced the attitudes of Western societies and of Western governments concerning Russian nationalism. Certain emigrants from the USSR and Eastern Europe – especially, it would seem, from the western Ukraine and from Poland – are wont to proclaim with considerable vehemence that Marxism-Leninism is only a mask for ethnic Russian imperialist designs. In their view there is little substantial difference between tsarist Russia and the Soviet Union. One result of this lobby's activities has been the startling omission of Russia from the list of Communist "captive nations," nations whose plight the U.S. Congress has been commemorating each July since 1959. In putting its imprimatur on the misguided views of this lobby, the Congress has been acting contrary to U.S. self-interest.

Conclusion

The Soviet Union, fueled by a "dead" yet still lethal ideology, continues its global expansion. Militarily, the regime represents a greater threat then ever before; politically, it continues to export its combustible ideology to Third World countries and to undermine, through subversion and disinformation, the countries of the West. At immense cost to its economies and to its spiritual resources, the West bustles about seeking to contain a relentless threat. Spawned by the fear of a nuclear exchange, pacifist challenges continually arise in the West, serving to erode its commitment to a credible deterrence and to military parity with the Soviet Union.

The death of ideology in the Soviet Union presents the West with a unique opportunity not merely to contain an expansionist adversary but to help halt its expansionism. Russian nationalism is rising up to contest and perhaps replace an enfeebled Marxism-Leninism. How the West reacts to this development is of no small consequence. If it chooses to launch a crusade against the nationalists, the West could retard what appears to be the natural evolution of the Soviet political system, thereby both prolonging the rule of Marxism-Leninism in the USSR and increasing the risk of war. Such a crusade could also so infuriate the nationalists that, if they were to come to power, any mutual accommodation would have to be postponed for decades. One hopes therefore that the West will choose to occupy at least a neutral position in the face of a political change that promises soon to occur in the USSR. The West could even, as has been suggested, choose to serve as a midwife of history and thereby help bring about a positive change that would benefit both itself and all the peoples of the USSR.

Part II

5

The Rise of Monarchist and Restorationist Sentiment in the Contemporary Soviet Union

> Granted that revolutions end in a return, not to the *status quo ante*, but to an equilibrium, a state of "normalcy" recognizably related to that of the old regime, then the end of the Russian Revolution should naturally be something a good deal more like the Russia of the Czars. . . .
>
> Crane Brinton
> *The Anatomy of Revolution*[89]

> The next political regime which is about to replace the decaying Bolshevik Jacobinism, will, according to the logic of all revolutionary processes, most certainly bear some restorationist features. . . .
>
> Alexander Shtromas
> *Political Change and Social Development*[90]

The question of social and political change is a vexing and complex one. It becomes especially so when it concerns the theoretical issue of the "evolution of revolutions." Do revolutions – whether the French and Puritan revolutions of the past, or the Russian and Iranian revolutions of our century – follow essentially similar evolutionary paths? As the quotes introducing this chapter indicate, scholars such as Crane

Brinton and Alexander Shtromas believe that they do. Other theorists, however, dispute that there are inevitabilities in history or that revolutions must, in mechanistic fashion, follow identical or similar paths. Still other theorists add that the phenomenon of totalitarianism injects a completely new element into the question of the evolution of revolutions and contend that Communist revolutions must of necessity evolve in ways dissimilar from non-Communist and nontotalitarian revolutions.

My intention is not to address the theoretical question of social and political change in the Soviet Union but rather to describe a development that has received insufficient attention on the part of Western observers: the marked rise of monarchist and restorationist sentiment in the contemporary USSR. What, if anything, this development may portend for the evolution of Russian revolution is something I will leave to political theorists and sociologists to elucidate. But the development itself clearly warrants detailed discussion.

An important sign concerning the growth of monarchist and restorationist sentiment during the Brezhnev period was the publication in 1972–1973 of Mark Kasvinov's study *Twenty-Three Steps Down* by the journal *Zvezda* (the title refers to the number of steps that Nicholas II and his family descended prior to being shot; it may also be a play on Nicholas's 23 years in power).[91] Although unquestionably an antimonarchist tract, the study (which was published in expanded book form by the publishing house Mysl' in 1979) offered a great deal of previously unavailable information concerning Nicholas, his family, and his reign.[92] The book caused a sensation among Soviet readers, who eagerly grasped at the crumbs of authentic information contained in Kasvinov's polemic; recent émigrés from the Soviet Union report that it was impossible to find the journal either in the kiosks or libraries, so heavy was readership demand for the usually pedestrian *Zvezda*.

Kasvinov's book purports to be aimed at distortions in the depiction of Nicholas and his rule introduced by White émigré authors and Western writers such as Robert Massie, author of *Nicholas and Alexandra* (a tacit admission that such writings circulate in *samizdat*). A more significant purpose, however, is indicated on page 21: "The author hopes that this book will be useful, especially for the youth. . . ."[93] There is an implicit suggestion that at least a part of the Soviet youth is in danger of falling into monarchist nets.

Realizing the limited appeal of the official ideology to his contemporaries, Kasvinov marshals a series of "Soviet patriotic" arguments to demonstrate the alleged perfidy of Nicholas, his consort, and his officials. Citing Maksim Gor'kii, he notes that the Romanovs did not possess any Russian blood. During World War I, he intimates, the empress served as a German spy. As for the tsar, he was a weakling, a liar, and, in Tolstoi's words, a "hidden executioner."[94] He most decidedly cannot be considered a martyr, as he seriously hoped to escape from imprisonment in Tobol'sk and Ekaterinburg.

The execution of the imperial family, Kasvinov maintains, was a regrettable necessity. "It does not follow," he stresses, "that what was done in the Ipat'ev House . . . made anyone happy either then or later."[95] Had Nicholas and his family not been shot, they could have fallen into the hands of the Whites or Germans. As for tsarism, it passed from the face of the earth, irrevocably, in 1917:

> The question was posed and taken out into the street: Should there be autocracy or not? History's answer: there should not. Tsarist Russia died.[96]

In places, Kasvinov's arguments could cause some confusion on the part of the uninitiated Western reader. Thus he insists at great length that a number of Nicholas's jailers, executioners, and those who gave the order for his execution were ethnic Russians. By doing so, he seeks to counter a widespread belief that the early Bolsheviks consisted mainly of non-Russians. At another point, he heatedly denies the existence of a Masonic "diabolism" (*d'iavolshchina*), whose aim was to seize power in the last days of Nicholas's reign.[97] It also seems noteworthy that the one minister of Nicholas II whom Kasvinov seems to respect is the Western-oriented Sergei Witte.

The appearance of Kasvinov's study showed that the author, the editors of *Zvezda* and of the Mysl' publishing house, and their protectors were troubled by the rise of monarchist and restorationist sentiment in the Soviet Union and decided to combat this unwelcome development through a hard-hitting exposé of Nicholas and his associates. One might add that, because he was Russia's last tsar, and because he and his family were brutally killed by the Bolsheviks, Nicholas II has become for contemporary Russians the preeminent symbol of the old order. His reign appears to exert a quasi-hypnotic effect on present-day Russians, who seem to sense, intuitively, that the period 1894 to 1917 is in some way critical for an understanding of the Soviet present and of the prospects for the future of the USSR. Thus writers ranging from neofascists, such as Valentin Pikul', the author of the notorious Soviet potboiler *At the Last Frontier*,[98] and Nikolai Iakovlev, author of *1 August 1914*,[99] to Nobel prizewinner Aleksandr Solzhenitsyn[100] and to the late "Westernizer" Andrei Amal'rik, who was writing a book on Rasputin at the time of his death,[101] are all fixated upon the reign of Emperor Nicholas II, a reign seen as somehow containing the key to the future of the Soviet Union.

In 1977, two dramatic events occurred that attested to the growth of monarchist sentiment in Soviet Russia: in the beginning of that year, the editor and assistant editor of the Leningrad journal *Avrora* were sacked from their posts for publishing a poem that lamented the imprisonment of the imperial family in Tobol'sk.[102] And in October, the large, structurally sound Ipat'ev House in Sverdlovsk, where Nicholas and his family were killed, was leveled on orders from the authorities.[103] The reason: the building had become a pilgrimage site.

In the previous year, 1976, Evgenii Vagin, formerly head of the ideological division of the underground military-political organization *VSKhSON*–the All-Russian Social-Christian Union for the Liberation of the People–was permitted, after serving a prison sentence, to emigrate to the West.[104] Now coeditor of the émigré journal *Veche*, of which 16 issues had appeared by the end of 1984, Vagin has emerged as one of the more influential monarchist spokesmen of the so-called third emigration. Shortly after emigrating in 1976, he wrote this concerning the rise of monarchist sentiment in the USSR:

> In the apartments of my acquaintances, young members of the intelligentsia – both those employed at Soviet institutions and those who have voluntarily given up warm spots in research institutes and laboratories and now work as loaders, yard-keepers, and stokers – one finds on their bookshelves, desks, and in the "red corner," often directly under the icons, pictures of Emperor Nicholas II, Empress Alexandra Fedorovna, and other members of the imperial family. Usually these photographs have been reproduced from old journals, books, and albums. . . . The possessors of these relics know well the geneology of the Romanov dynasty and also the "present situation," if one may so put it. Some of them have photographs of Grand Prince Vladimir Kirillovich; others would like to have a portrait of the Grand Princess Maria Vladimirovna.[105]

And there is this account by the gifted poet Iurii Kublanovskii, a 1982 émigré from the Soviet Union, whose poems appeared in the *Metropol'* collection and have received high praise from Joseph Brodsky. When one visits the home of a member of the nomenklatura elite, Kublanovskii writes, one is likely to see "photographs of our Cyclops [Brezhnev et al.]" on the walls. But: "Let us turn into the room of the son, here one finds a votive lamp, a photo of the last tsar and empress, a simple icon of St. Seraphim of Sarov. . . . "[106]

The Western observer may be inclined to dismiss such restorationist sentiment as a faddist and adolescent, or post-adolescent, rebellion against the values of the older generation. But it is noteworthy that Kublanovskii himself – an educated and cultured man – is a convinced monarchist. Concerning the canonization of the imperial family and the new Russian martyrs in 1981, he writes, for example:

> The glorification of the New Russian Martyrs by the Russian Church Abroad was received by us with joy. The sermon of Archbishop Antonii of Geneva [broadcast over the foreign radio] was transcribed from tape recorder to tape recorder. . . . [107]

Justifying this glorification, he observes:

> I see clearly the state weakness of the last tsar. . . . Nevertheless, the whole path of Nicholas and his family – from the February Revolution to the Urals – was undoubtedly a way of the cross, a sacrificial path, inspiring religious veneration. . . . In this sense, it is completely "traditional" for the understanding of martyrdom. . . . [108]

That monarchist and restorationist sentiment has penetrated the ranks of the Soviet cultural elite becomes clear from a reading of Evgenii Evtushenko's 1981 novel *Iagodnye mesta* (Berry Places).[109] Evtushenko, who is a vehement antimonarchist, introduces into his novel a certain "ideologist-essayist," who publishes in Soviet literary journals and is surrounded by sycophantic admirers. In his home, which is adorned with ancient icons, a church bell, and a photograph of Nicholas II making the rounds of his officers, the essayist proclaims: "The path of Russia is in an enlightened autocracy, united with Orthodoxy."[110] "For the tsar, the homeland, and the faith . . . ," he intones, while proposing toasts to the "Russian officer corps." His admiring followers read poems about "Holy Russia."

Evtushenko's portrait of the essayist, while obviously modeled in part on *derevenshchik* writer Vladimir Soloukhin, is a composite (unlike the essayist, Soloukhin does not, for example, have an Old Believer beard) that seeks to embrace a tendency in Soviet letters and art.[111] Although a vitriolic caricature, Evtushenko's essayist serves to demonstrate the existence of monarchist and restorationist sentiment among influential elements of the Soviet cultural elite. The perceived outreach of these elements to the Soviet military is also noteworthy.

Whatever the Western reader may think of monarchism, Vagin, Kublanovskii, and Evtushenko's essayist are not isolated eccentrics. Restorationist sentiment is indeed markedly on the rise today in the USSR, while monarchism is a serious political philosophy to a number of Soviet intellectuals and may even have potential mass appeal. If the West has generally failed to take note of this, the Soviet authorities have been more discerning; hence the publication of Kasvinov's antimonarchist tract and the leveling of the Ipat'ev House in 1977.

Perhaps no cultural medium has had as much influence on the rise of monarchist sentiment in the USSR as that of film, which, of course, reaches a mass audience. Since the mid-1960s, at least three films have been produced that deal directly with Nicholas II and his tragedy: *His Majesty's Crown* (*Korona Ego Velichestva*); *Before the Judgment of History*, narrated by Vasilii Shul'gin;[112] and *Agony* (*Agoniia*), directed by Elem Klimov. The last-named film, completed in 1975, has yet to be released for general distribution; it was, however, screened at the Moscow Film Festival in 1981.[113] Also noteworthy are Soviet films about the White movement that depict White officers and soldiers in a positive light (the film *Two Comrades* would be an example).[114] Although, historically speaking, many Whites were not monarchists, there is a tendency today in the USSR to consider them to have been.

Writing in 1982, Evgenii Vagin recalled:

> I well remember the enthusiasm which was elicited in the cinemas . . . when *White* officers appeared on the screen. . . . I even remember the words of several "White Guard" songs, which were sung in such films and then received broad dissemination.[115]

Another recent émigré and monarchist, Aleksandr Udodov, observes:

> The White struggle in Russia has not been forgotten. Even the tone of Soviet films in recent years has changed markedly. Caricatures on the White officers have disappeared. . . . As a concession to public opinion, the White officers are shown as intelligent, valiant, and honest opponents. The sympathy of the viewers is entirely on their side.[116]

Recent émigré Andrei Korzhinskii, who served in the Soviet armed forces during the 1970s, reports that such films are especially popular among Soviet army officers, who yearn for the "good old times" of the prerevolutionary officer corps and contemptuously dismiss the present Soviet leaders as "political prostitutes."[117] A final testimony concerning contemporary sympathies for the Whites is this open letter, written by the great-grandson of a Red Army commander. The reader's indulgence is requested so that the document may be quoted in full:

> **An Open Letter to Participants in the White Movement**
>
> I am not certain that this letter will succeed in reaching you. There are fewer and fewer of you among the living. But, perhaps contrary to sound sense, I am sending it in the hope that it will reach at least someone.
>
> I am 22 years old and live in Moscow, where I was born. Like all my peers, I have since childhood heard how the heroic Red Army defeated the White Guardists and brought freedom to the people. Like everyone else, I believed this. That is how they educate us here: on the heroism of the Reds and the vileness of the Whites. Recently, however, strange things have been happening. In the milieu of my friends, the usual values have shifted. In our conversations and in the songs which we sing,

it is not the Reds who come out as heroes. Our hearts, our sympathy are on the side of the Whites.

The Red Army defended freedom? But then where is it? (Not the army, of course; it remains in place. But where is freedom?)

Those of us who have not yet become drunkards are beginning seriously to think. You read a newspaper: everything appears to be fine – there is happiness, equality, enthusiasm, freedom. You look around you: everything is different – there is drunkenness, injustice, falsehood, and servitude. Of course far from all of us are prepared to speak about this aloud, and even to admit it to ourselves can be difficult. But somewhere, if only subconsciously, almost all of us think this way.

Already the generation of our parents made the hero of the civil war, Division Commander Vasilii Ivanovich Chapaev, a laughingstock and the butt of obscene jokes. There it is: the judgment of the people.

By contrast, however, the officers of the White Army have more and more become for us a model of honesty and nobility. It is difficult to get the books of Mikhail Bulgakov.[118] They do not give out newspapers from those years in libraries. The history textbooks unquestionably lie. But despite this lack of information (or perhaps thanks to it), there has been formed in the folklore of urban youth the romantic image of a White officer, aware of his doom but courageously meeting death for the right cause.

It is probably difficult for you to imagine this scene. It is the 1980s. Evening. A crowded Moscow apartment. Someone picks up a guitar and begins to sing softly. Others pick up the tune. It might be a new "underground" song or even a legally permitted song from an old film, but interpreted in a new way:

> There are no longer enough of us to fill
>   ranks of eight
> And heroes are bored by Soviet jargon
> And the last autumn sews crosses
> On the rubbed-out gold of our shoulder
>   boards. . . .

And each of us mentally sees himself in the place of that [White] officer and begins to ponder. . . .

Your titles and names sound exalted and moving to our ears. Here are the heroes of a new song, one of the most popular now at our parties:

Don't despair, Lieutenant Golitsyn,
Cornet Obolenskii, pour the wine.[119]

It is now the fashion when signing one's name to use the old orthography.

I decided to write this letter so that, perhaps at the sunset of your days, it would be pleasant for you to learn that you have not been forgotten, that long decades of Soviet propaganda have not been able to expunge you from the popular memory; that the youth in Russia see in you knights without fear or reproach and deem that you did not struggle in vain.

We are the grandsons of Red Army men and Red commissars (I myself am the great-grandson of the commander of a Red regiment). Looking around and pondering, we begin with horror to realize into what an abyss the Bolsheviks have led the people. Looking back into the dark past, covered with lies, we come to this conclusion:

Time, history, and perhaps even a majority of the Russian people were on the side of the Communists.

Truth, honor, and Russia were on your side.

We regret that it was not you who won. We do not accuse you. Probably you did all you could. We are thankful to you for that.

If you believe in God, pray for us!

December 1982[120]

At the root of contemporary monarchist sentiment, and of sympathy for the White movement, lies a revulsion for the seedy, inefficient, unaesthetic, mean-spirited Soviet present. Contemporary monarchists, writes Mikhail Gol'dshtein, "like to compare the mores (*byt*) and economic life of Russia under the old and the new regimes."[121] In a sense, one has to do with a quest for a lost ideal, with a retrospective utopia.

Imperial Russia does not look at all bad when compared with Brezhnev's, Andropov's, or Chernenko's Soviet Union. "Monarchism," Vagin writes,

> is not simply a political ideology. It is a holistic world-experience (*tselostnoe miroperezhivanie*), with deep roots in the popular soul. The pious attitude toward the memory of the tsar-martyr, which not long ago induced the authorities to level the Ipat'ev house, testifies to the attractiveness of the "idea" of monarchy. . . . A purely political idea cannot today so easily "win over the masses," who have been repeatedly deceived by attractive promises.[122]

In the struggle of ideas in contemporary Russia, the "monarchist variant," Vagin believes, has its advantages.

To return to what was said at the beginning of this essay, the obvious growth of monarchist and restorationist sentiment during the Brezhnev era is a development that Western analysts would ignore to their peril. The significance of the development for the evolution of the Russian Revolution is a subject to be discussed and debated by specialists in social and political change. Whatever its significance, it seems clear, however, that the development should neither be overlooked nor cursorily dismissed.

6

Two Films for the Soviet Masses

The leadership of the Soviet Union has recognized the political and mobilizational importance of film from the beginning. Lenin was alert to the propaganda uses to which the fledgling art could be put, while Stalin sought heavy handedly to manipulate the talents of even such geniuses as Sergei Eisenstein. If the Communist Party and Western film critics have generally paid close attention to the development of this "most important art," the same cannot be said of Western sovietologists, who have traditionally paid it little heed.[123] Literature and, to some extent, painting have been combed and scrutinized for clues to shifting political currents, but film has been largely ignored.[124] Because film often reaches a mass audience in the USSR, such a dismissive attitude can hardly be justified.

The Khrushchev years, with their clear-cut division of Soviet intellectuals into liberals and hardliners, were relatively open to Western understanding and analysis. The Brezhnev period, on the other hand, was a time of deepening political and social complexity. During the 18 years of Brezhnev's reign, the official ideology of Marxism-Leninism suffered significant attrition among the populace, while surging currents of nationalism and religion – or a combination of the two – made important inroads into Soviet society. Because of the complex and partially sub rosa nature of these processes, Western observers often had difficulty in seeing and in conceptualizing what was taking place. Like a seismograph, however, Soviet films that have enjoyed mass popularity have been recording the shiftings and tremors occurring in the political and social life of the USSR over the past 20 years.

Recently two films broke all records in domestic attendance: *Moscow Does Not Believe in Tears* (*Moskva slezam ne verit*, 1980) and *Siberiade* (*Sibiriada*, 1979), seen by 100 million and 80 million viewers respectively.[125] "One hundred million is almost the entire adult population of the USSR!" a demographer exclaimed upon hearing these figures, and indeed the reasons for the unprecedented popularity of these two films should be of interest to all Soviet analysts, and indeed to all those concerned with U.S.-Soviet relations. The editor of the prestigious Soviet film journal *Isskustvo kino*, Evgenii Surkov, recently wrote:

> Through a film we are able to enter that social milieu to which it is directed. We can draw close to an understanding of the moral condition of society, and of the expectations, hopes, ideals, and needs of the viewers. One can study these subjects by means of questionnaires, polls, etc. But one can also do so by proceeding from the depths of the film itself.[126]

Lacking access to Soviet questionnaires and polls—though we shall make use of an interesting roundtable discussion published in *Iskusstvo kino* and of excerpts from readers' letters appearing in *Sovetskii ekran*—one must of necessity follow Surkov's advice and proceed from the "depths" of the films themselves.[127]

Moscow Does Not Believe in Tears, which was directed by Vladimir Men'shov, won an American Academy Award in 1980. Despite this recognition, it has often been dismissed by Western (as well as Soviet) film critics as a soap opera, a lowbrow film catering to the masses. That the film is intentionally geared to the masses cannot be doubted. "I made this film," Men'shov stated during the roundtable discussion of *Moscow* sponsored by *Iskusstvo kino*, "having in view a clear-cut audience: the mass viewer."[128]

Although the director intended his film to be a picture for the masses, the Soviet film industry apparently expected little from it. No special steps were taken to ensure *Moscow's* success; no flyers were issued; no ads were made on radio or television. "Simply the picture appeared on the screens, and for months now the lines for tickets have not dried up. . . ."[129] "Everyone has come together in the lines for tickets – academicians and carpenters, heads of families and green youths."[130] In the two theaters in Moscow that showed the film, 1,860,000 viewers queued up to see the picture in the first two months it played, breaking all previous records.[131]

Moscow, which opens in the year 1958, examines the fate of three young women from the provinces living in a crowded workers' dormitory in the capital. Katia Tikhomirova, the central protagonist, is a bright, decent, career-oriented young woman. Liuda, her roommate, is ambitious in her personal life, seeking to "win the lottery" by marrying a present or future member of the Soviet elite. The third roommate, Tosia, is, by contrast, close to her peasant roots, in love with a humble worker, a rock of humanity, Kolia.

The film follows the lives of the three women over the next two decades. Tosia and Kolia have three sons, their marriage prospers, and they are able to spend time in the countryside, surrounded by fecund fruit trees in an atmosphere of harmony and contentment. Their life is depicted as a kind of idyll. Referring to Tosia and Kolia's marriage, a female participant in the *Iskusstvo kino* roundtable discussion observed:

> I consider that a true, friendly family is a fortress of human happiness. . . . One can count on Kolia and Tosia – they will not let you down. . . . And the fact that Tosia has raised three beautiful sons – this is also a female exploit. Who does not know what it means in our difficult time to raise three children, to have a family, to preserve in it an atmosphere of pure and dedicated friendship![132]

The fate of the Russian family, threatened by numerous social and demographic factors, including a precipitous decline in fertility, rampant alcoholism, mass migration from village to city, an increasing divorce rate, and the necessity for both husband and wife to work, is a major, indeed perhaps the central, concern of the film.

Tosia's social-climbing roommate, Liuda, decides early in the film that she must catch either an academician or an engineer. She catches neither but does capture a celebrated hockey player, Serezha Gurin, who has traveled abroad with his team. Unfortunately for the marriage, every Soviet hockey fan who encounters Serezha insists on buying him a drink, and soon the gifted athlete has become an alcoholic. The childless marriage ends in divorce, its only reminder being Serezha's periodic visits to beg for money. The theme of alcoholism and its ruinous effects on the modern Russian family is an important focus of the film.

Katia occupies a middle ground between Tosia and Liuda. While still very young, she is gotten pregnant by Rudolf, a flashy technician in the Soviet TV industry. Under pressure from his mother, who despises Katia's peasant background – though the mother herself has only recently emerged from the village – Rudolf refuses Katia marriage, with the result that she is cast adrift, encumbered by a baby daughter, Sasha. The subject of class barriers in Soviet society is another problem examined by the film.

Through grit, application, and determination, Katia eventually manages to climb the managerial ladder and becomes the director of a textile factory. She drives a Zhiguli and possesses a comfortable apartment. Her success leads to her being featured on Soviet TV (the occasion, predictably, for a painful encounter with Rudolf, who has, in the meantime, passed through two unsuccessful marriages). Thus Katia is a symbol of the upwardly mobile Soviet female, an image much touted in the Soviet media. Yet, as the film clearly shows, at age 40 she is far from happy. A tawdry affair with a married man cannot fill the void. As a roundtable discussant commented, the film "prompts us to meditate on what female happiness is, and where its sources lie."[133]

By chance, Katia encounters Georgii Ivanovich (Goga), a fitter at a scientific institute, on a train. Goga's social status is considerably beneath that of Katia, though he is constantly praised by his superiors, many the possessors of Ph.D.'s, for his "golden hands." Goga is tough, yet responsible and compassionate. The man, he asserts, must be the boss in the home; yet he pitches in energetically with the housework, does much of the cooking, wraps Katia in a blanket when she becomes cold at a picnic. Similarly, he conscientiously discharges his substitute-father's duties when Sasha's boyfriend is threatened by neighborhood hoodlums. (The problem of youth delinquency and its causes are examined by the film.) The intrepid Goga, however, runs away when he learns that Katia outranks him socially, and it takes all of Kolia's caring humanity to effect a reconciliation.

Beneath its soap opera veneer, *Moscow* engages in significant social commentary. As we have seen, the fate of the endangered Russian family is a centerpiece of the film. At one point, Katia talks to the director of a Soviet "dating bureau," whose job it is to bring isolated and lonely Soviet men and women together. The woman, who is idealistic and sincere, complains about the state of male-female relations in the USSR – about social conditions that have led to a precipitous drop in the birthrate, to poor work habits, and to alcoholism. All Soviet men want to do, she grouses, is drink and watch TV. (The film emphasizes the numbing social effects of modern TV.)

A significant issue raised by the film is that of Western borrowings. *Moscow* is not xenophobic on this question, but it does articulate a nationalist view that Russians are too enamored of the West, particularly of the superficial aspects of its culture. The city of Moscow of 1958 is shown to be wild over a French film festival, while 20 years later Katia's daughter is rather too keen on ear-shattering Western pop music. The fashion of giving one's children foreign names is also implicitly criticized. "We used to have a lot of Rudolfs and Eduards," Katia tells Rudolf, who has since, we learn, changed his name to Rodion, "an ancient Russian name."

The participants in the *Iskusstvo kino* roundtable discussion were nearly unanimous in their enthusiasm for *Moscow Does Not Believe in Tears*. "This film is life itself, and the heroes are we ourselves," enthused Raisa Lifanova, the head of a section at the central telegraph office, and her sentiments were uniformly echoed.[134] "No falsehood [in the film]! For me that is very important," exclaimed Elena Kuritskaia, an engineer at a Moscow watch factory.[135] Similar enthusiasm is expressed in the excerpts from readers' letters published in the popular screen magazine *Sovetskii ekran*.[136] "The film touches those problems and those human relations that are often met with in daily life," wrote 32 signatories to a collective letter. A woman reader wrote in: "My daughter and I went to the film *Moscow Does Not Believe in Tears*. No, that is not precise. We paid a visit to dear people close to our hearts." "As if spellbound," recalled another reader, "I have been walking about for several days under the influence of this film. I look around and see the kind eyes of its heroes. . . . "

The use of the adjective *dobryi* (kind or good) by the last-cited correspondent is not fortuitous. As Vera Alentova, the actress who played Katia in the film, remarked during the roundtable discussion: "We wanted very much to produce a kind (*dobryi*) film–kind in the sense that kind, good people live and act in it. . . . "[137] For the film's director, Men'shov, the fact that "the picture gives birth to warm feelings" in its viewers both corresponds to his intentions and is gratifying. He further points out that the film advocates tolerance for human foibles: "In my film, I do not judge any of the heroes."[138]

Almost in passing, Men'shov provided another key to the film's success: "I think that in this film I caught the Russian national character. It is sensed both in the situations and in the actions and in the manner of acting."[139] It should be noted that Men'shov here employed the term *Russian* national character, not Soviet. His film is intentionally geared to the concerns – the hopes, anxieties, and fears – of the dominant nationality of the Soviet federation.

Faced with *Moscow's* overwhelming success, the Communist Party, which had not made a special effort to promote or publicize the film, decided to coopt it. Boris Griaznov, first secretary of the Frunze district party organization in Moscow, praised the film, incongruously, for being "permeated with our Soviet Communist spirit. . . ."[140] The optimism pervading *Moscow* strikes him as a notable Communist trait. Indeed, the picture reminds him of the Stalinist classic of the 1930s, *Chapaev*, and he pledges to make use of it for propaganda work with the masses.

Griaznov, of course, is wide of the mark. *Moscow* has nothing in common with the senescent official ideology. The optimism pervading the film is that of Dostoevskii and of much of the nineteenth century Russian literary canon, not that of the official ideology. It is an optimism that contends that one must endure, that one must accept suffering, and that, when it seems too late, one may then find meaning and love. Kindness, refraining from judgment, acceptance of suffering – these are all anathema to Soviet Marxism-Leninism. In instances where the film does display ideological proclivities, it is in a Russian nationalist rather than Marxist direction. To the degree that one of Men'shov's aims in the film was to grasp and convey the Russian national character, he seems to have succeeded, and the masses responded by the millions.

The second most heavily attended picture in the history of Soviet cinema was Andrei Mikhalkov-Konchalovskii's *Siberiade*, the winner of a special prize at the Cannes Film Festival in 1979. Its success was even more surprising than that of *Moscow*. Eighty million viewers thronged to see a difficult modern film employing a complicated pattern of symbols and imagery, with few concessions made to mass taste.

Siberiade recounts the history of three generations of the Ustuzhanin family, whose roots lie in the remote western Siberian village of Elan' (a word phonetically related to the Russian word for deer, *olen'*). The film begins in the year 1909 and concludes in the 1960s, encompassing a half-century of Russian and Soviet historical experience.

Afanasii Ustuzhanin, the grandfather, is a driven man who, to the alternating consternation and amusement of his fellow villagers, takes upon himself the task of cutting a road through the dense, often swampy taiga surrounding Elan'. Afanasii embodies man's innate Promethean impulses; the forest moans as his skilled ax topples huge trees, while a wildcat who crosses his path is trussed up and suspended from a tree. Ustuzhanin is not an evil man, but he is driven by a compulsion to remake the earth in his own image. At the moment of his death, we see him lying drunk in the forest with his face resting on an anthill, whose denizens move across his face. The Dostoevskian anthill reference and the allusion to the Soviet plague of alcoholism will recur throughout the film.[141]

Afanasii's son, Kolia, born in 1897, is of a generation that helped make the Bolshevik revolution. While a young man, he falls in love with a fiery village girl, Anastasia Solomina – the daughter of wealthy peasants – is rejected by her (she marries another village lad, Filka, instead), and then is unexpectedly chosen again, whereupon the two flee from the village into the cauldron of war, revolution, and civil war.

After several years, Kolia returns to his native village breathing the fire of revolution and social change. Since boyhood, Kolia has been swayed by the rhetoric of class hatred that favored his family, poor peasants, over such wealthy villagers as the Solomins, even though the Solomins are hardworking and disciplined. Kolia comes back to the village without his wife, who perished in the civil war – White Cossacks doused her with alcohol and set her on fire – but accompanied by his young son, Alesha, a revolutionary fanatic. With Kolia's arrival, the flames of class discord begin to race through the previously peaceful settlement. Ideology, *Siberiade* shows, poisons human relationships, which are difficult enough without it. Anastasia's brother, Spiridon, vows revenge against Kolia for his sister's death, and this hatred is deepened by ideological animosity. Spiridon believes neither in the bright future touted by the regime nor in the wisdom of Comrade Stalin.

Like his late father, Kolia Ustuzhanin embodies the Promethean impulse; ideology, however, serves to strengthen and magnify this tendency. At one point, he drags his son out into the swamps in quest of the semimagical spot that the villagers call the "devil's patch" (*chertova griva*). When Alesha nonchalantly tosses away a cigarette, the swamp bursts into flames, anticipating the inferno at the picture's end. The black-and-white film that Konchalovskii employs for the swamp scene underscores the nightmarish quality of this episode.

Empowered by the regime to bring order to his native village, Kolia eventually decides to arrest Spiridon, his brother-in-law, and send him down river under guard. He later admits to regret over this action, for Kolia has not forgotten the simplicity of village relationships, the fact that all are brothers and sisters. Shortly before Spiridon's arrest, the two of them join in singing the magnificent peasant songs that have existed for a millenium. (Anastasia, too, had sung these songs while working in the fields.) Upon his release from prison, Spiridon returns to Elan' and, in the year 1932, brutally murders his brother-in-law. The horror on young Alesha's face as he confronts his uncle with his father's blood on his hands is that of Russia's new "time of troubles." Alesha flees the village, swearing revenge.

When Alesha returns shortly before the outbreak of World War II, he learns, to his distress and disappointment, that Spiridon has been given a lengthy prison sentence and is beyond reach. While en route to Elan', he encounters an old man, the *vechnyi ded* or "eternal grandfather," sprung from the Russian lives of saints and fairy tales, who lives surrounded by birds, bees, and a convivial bear. Alesha's frenetic pace while in the grip of passion contrasts with the grandfather's serenity. Snatches from the Orthodox church services come to the old man's lips; he sings pointedly about the Biblical prodigal son while Alesha is temporarily living under his roof.

In Elan', Alesha encounters the village girl, Taia, who is intrigued by his record player and by the one tango record that he plays over and over on it. Strange sounds and rhythms are impinging upon Elan's organic harmony and domesticity. (The role of music in the film is central.)

Throughout *Siberiade*, the natural life of the isolated village, frozen in time, has been contrasted with the cacophonous rush of events in the world outside. Employing black-and-white documentary footage, speeded up to catch the headlong pace of events, the film offers us snatches of World War I, of Lenin orating to the masses, of revolution and civil war, and of Stalin's sinister rise to power. Men are depicted rushing about frantically like the swarming ants that covered Afanasii Ustuzhanin's face at the moment of his death. And always there are explosions. At the beginning of the film, we are shown a Siberian revolutionary who passes through the village of Elan' fleeing from the tsarist police. The revolutionary, in thrall to a vision of a future "City of the Sun" that he and his fellow utopians will construct, is idealistic and gentle, almost seraphic, and Kolia Ustuzhanin is drawn to him. But the bomb that he throws at the police who have come to arrest him is far from gentle, and it reverberates with increasing force throughout the film, clearing the way for the holocaust at the picture's end.

World War II arrives in Elan' in the form of a recruiters' steamer that winds its way upriver to take the Siberian young men off to war. The people of Elan' know nothing of the cataclysm shaking Eurasia; the village's one wireless has long been in disrepair. "Didn't we already fight the Germans?" they ask in perplexity. Though legally too young to enlist, Alesha begs the officers to take him, and, with regret, they do. Taia watches him leave on the steamer and vows to await his return.

Bombs, bombs, bombs. An incessant tramp of soldiers' feet. Huge mechanical engines of destruction soaring in the air and lumbering about on the earth. We encounter Alesha amid a scene of desolation and destruction – conveyed in black-and-white – dragging a severely wounded officer to safety (we later learn that it is Filka, Anastasia's first husband). All around is fetid water, dotted by shell fragments, a scene recalling Alesha's dream-like journey with his father into the swamps surrounding Elan' in quest of the devil's patch. As Alesha crawls along dragging Filka in an improvised sling, huge tanks roar past like modern-day dinosaurs, symbolizing the widespread mechanical destruction. Fortunately, the tanks are "ours," and Alesha and Filka are saved; but the tanks remain a dreadful presage of the forces man can unleash upon man.

Finally, we come to the 1960s and to Alesha's last return to his native village. This time he is not on a mission of revenge (he plants an affectionate kiss on the decrepit Spiridon's bald pate), but to build a "City of the Sun" complete with high-rises and the appurtenances of "civilization." In the years since the end of the war, Alesha has become an oil prospector and is now a valued member of a drilling team, headed by the Azerbaidzhani, Tofik from Baku, whose mustachioed face, dark complexion, and harsh Russian intonations recall Stalin, whose image on posters and in documentary footage has been associated throughout the film with forced industrialization and breakneck modernization. (One should stress that the link between Tofik and Stalin is symbolic; in his relations with his fellow workers, Tofik is shown to be a decent individual.) The drilling team is in Elan' to find oil; if they fail to do so, the area will be flooded by the construction of a large hydroelectric dam on the nearby river. Alesha's first symbolic act upon arriving at the village is to drive his vehicle through the finely wrought gates of Elan', knocking one of them off its hinges.

In the village, Alesha encounters Taia, whom he is able to recall only with great difficulty. He is stunned when she tells him that she waited for him for years before finally taking a job on the steamer which plies its way up and down the river. While working on the steamer, she, too, has made contact with modern civilization. Both Taia and Alesha have contemporary tastes in music; the ditties they sing are trite and vulgar, unlike the melodious folksongs sung by their parents.

They are also taken with the Gypsy songs sung by a former convict who strolls about the village with a guitar.

Soon we see Alesha crashing through the swamps in an amphibious vehicle (reminiscent of the tanks that roared past him during the war) in quest of the devil's patch and of oil. His route takes him past a swarming anthill. There then takes place a haunting scene – conveyed in black-and-white – in which he stops at a decaying hut near an abandoned oil rig that had belonged to earlier oil prospectors. The fetid hut, with a decomposing poster of Stalin on the door urging the Soviet people on to new achievements and with its floorboards collapsing into the water below brings nightmarish visions of his murdered father. Such forebodings soon disappear, however, amid the utter ecstasy with which Alesha and his fellow workers, driven by the indefatigable Tofik, proceed about their quest for oil. The footage of the oil-drilling equipment in action – so different from the early Eisenstein's love affair with machinery – creates an ominous impression, as do the shouts and frenetic scurrying about of the workers, thrilled with their control over nature. The violent insertion of the drill into the earth is clearly depicted as a kind of rape, and the eternal grandfather's shudder as the drill penetrates is noteworthy.

One day, unexpectedly, oil comes gushing out of the ground. Alesha, who had been about to leave the village and whose offer of marriage had been turned down by Taia, though she may be bearing his child – or is it Tofik's?), rushes to help. There is a moment of overwhelming exuberance as Tofik and his wondrous machines seek to harness the elemental outpouring from the earth. Then, suddenly, the gusher catches fire, and an inferno ensues. A fellow worker is trapped under some machinery, and Alesha rushes to a crane to lift it. He succeeds, but the crane catches fire, and Alesha, like his mother before him, perishes amid flames. The village graveyard catches fire as well and burns to the accompaniment of religious choral music. The cross over Afanasii Ustuzhanin's grave is shown burning. Huge white birds, covered with oil, catch fire and flap helplessly about the graveyard, in a dramatic culmination of the film's use of bird imagery. (Earlier, Taia had prevented Alesha from shooting a swan; the eternal grandfather had been shown surrounded by birds; and the feuding of Kolia and Spiridon had been compared to the squabbling of two small chicks.) Fire, not flood, has come to Elan', whose place-name symbolizes the precarious state of the Russian environment, and of Russia herself.

At the film's end, Filka, Anastasia's first husband, now in a politically exalted position as a provincial party first secretary, returns to the village for the second time. Earlier he had come to Elan' while the drilling was progressing and had met Alesha, whom he recognized as Anastasia's son. Thinking of his former wife on that occasion, he realized that he should have stood up for her. (Does, one wonders, Konchalovskii have Dostoevskii's frequent symbolic use of the name Anastasia [which means "resurrection" in Greek] in mind here?) As he visits the burned-out, gutted village graveyard at the film's end, Filka experiences a sadness that links him to the grief of his fellow villagers. Filka is a good man, still close, despite his station, to the simplicity of relations characterizing the villagers. But does he realize what has happened, what must be done?

As such Western filmmakers as Jon Voight have recognized,[142] *Siberiade* is an extraordinary achievement, arguably the best Soviet film of the post-Stalin period. Using Dostoevskian symbolic patterns, the film recounts the searingly painful story of Russia's "terrible years." Something, the picture suggests, is out of joint in modern civilization; some elementary truths have been ignored or forgotten. And it asks important questions: Can the values of the traditional village – neighborliness, mutual love, respect for the natural environment – withstand a crescendo crash of loud music, raucous machinery, and bombs, bombs, bombs? Or is it to be the devil's patch and a fiery inferno? On the symbolic level, Konchalovskii appears to hedge his answer: Taia may be bearing Alesha's child, and the Ustuzhanin (read: Russia) line may not be extinct, or she may be carrying Tofik's seed, in which case there is no hope. The questions permeating *Siberiade*, it should be noted, are universal as well as specifically Russian. Eighty million Soviet viewers flocked to the picture to form their own opinions. As for the regime, it seems to have made no attempt to co-opt the film, for obvious reasons.[143]

To sum up, Soviet viewers were drawn, en masse, to two recent films that suggest that the USSR – and indeed all of Western civilization – may be in thrall to destructive processes. Modern urban life and the vaunted scientific and technical revolution may be leading humanity to an irreversible cataclysm. The violation of the natural environment and the demographic and social degeneration of ethnic Russians are seen as symptoms of the disease. The solution to the problem, both Men'shov and Konchalovskii seem to suggest, is somehow connected with the fast-disappearing traditional Russian village – not in the sense of turning back the clock, but rather of grafting age-old morals and mores onto the lives of deracinated modern Russians.

It is noteworthy that the late West German specialist, Klaus Mehnert, came to similar conclusions in his recently published study, *The Russians and Their Favorite Books*, based on extensive interviews conducted in the USSR in 1981, 1982, and early 1983 and devoted to the 24 most popular fiction writers among contemporary ethnic Russians. Summing up the results of his ambitious public opinion poll, Mehnert writes: "One of the two topics appearing most persistently in the Russians' works of fiction [the other is the Second World War] is never found on Western best-seller lists: . . . the village . . . This is strange. The USSR is one of the most industrialized countries in the world.[144] Seeking to explain this phenomenon, he observes:

> Millions of Russians find it easier to identify with the village they came from . . . than with the miles of prefabricated apartment blocks in the cities or the smokestacks of the highly eulogized giants of industry. Like many people in the West, the Russians have begun to feel that human values are being sacrificed on the altar of progress, that modern cities are by no means better

> than the old-fashioned villages, that, in fact, preindustrial life possessed many advantages. . . . Ecology came late to Russia, but this movement can now be felt there, and the "back to nature" it propounds also means "back to the village" and even "back to Siberia."[145]

In addition to antiurbanism and anti-Prometheanism, Russian nationalism – of an inward-directed kind not easily melded with the official ideology – is clearly discernible in the two films. That this sentiment has become a powerful contemporary force was demonstrated by the remarkable success of two month-long exhibits of canvases by Russian nationalist painter Il'ia Glazunov held in Moscow in 1978 and Leningrad in 1979.

To conclude, behind the military-industrial titan with its hard, uncompromising ideology, which many of us in the West see as the USSR (and which, in a certain real sense, *is* the USSR), one catches glimpses of another Russia – a humane, introspective, personalistic, spiritual Russia. In inchoate fashion, through the choice of the films they flock to see, the paintings they stand in long lines to view, and the books they wait for years to read, Soviet citizens are sending an important message to their leaders, and to us in the West. God grant that this new, emerging Russia – which in many ways is the old Russia of Dostoevskii and Tolstoi – be permitted to break through to the surface. The Soviet masses are speaking, and their voices should be heard.

7

Mnogaia Leta: Advocate of a Russian Church-Soviet State Concordat*

In 1974, the important Russian nationalist *samizdat* journal *Veche* was suppressed by the KGB after a three-year existence and its editor, Vladimir Osipov, sentenced to eight years in the camps. Although this has not been sufficiently understood in the West, *Veche* represented a publication of considerable political significance, serving as a sounding board for most strands of contemporary ethnic Russian nationalism. In this respect, the title was most appropriate: the word *veche* refers to the medieval popular assembly. Today *Veche* remains the unsurpassed source for every student of this important ideological current in the USSR, a trend, moreover, that continues to have sympathizers in the ranks of the party-state elite and the Soviet military.

The KGB has apparently resolved not to permit sequentially numbered Russian nationalist *samizdat* journals to appear in the future. Thus *Obshchina* (Community), a publication of the Moscow-based Religio-Philosophical Seminar headed by Aleksandr Ogorodnikov, now in prison, was severely harassed and persecuted by the authorities, as was the journal

*This essay is an updated and slightly revised version of an article appearing in *Religion in Communist Lands* 11, no. 2 (1983): 146–150. Reprinted with permission.

Maria, organ of a most interesting Russian Orthodox women's club, whose leaders were expelled to the West. (Others have since been arrested.)

Given this situation, it was with some surprise that one learned of the appearance in 1980 and 1981 of the *samizdat* almanac, *Mnogaia leta*,[146] edited by the conservative nationalist, Gennadii Shimanov. Each issue of the almanac contained approximately 200 pages. One wondered why the regime would permit Shimanov and his authors' collective (Felix Karelin and Vladimir Ibragimov being the most noteworthy contributors) to engage in such activity.

An examination of *Mnogaia leta*, which is now available in the West, suggests an answer to this question.[147] Whereas *Veche*, while professing its "loyalty" to the Soviet state, had focused on points of conflict between the regime and Russian nationalists – for example, the widespread and continuing destruction of Russian historical and cultural monuments, the rape of the environment, demographic and social threats to the well-being of ethnic Russians, the persecution of the Russian Church – *Mnogaia leta* studiously downplays and often ignores such problems, concentrating instead on points of common interest between what Shimanov calls "conservative Orthodoxy" and the Soviet state.[148] This orientation strikes one as more than a matter of tactics, though tactical considerations are undoubtedly involved; the almanac's authors sincerely believe that the principal danger to Russia and the Russian Orthodox Church is not the Brezhnev regime (the second issue appeared before Brezhnev's death) but other "forces." Moreover, they seem certain that the USSR is evolving, ineluctably, in a positive, hopeful direction.

When one recalls that both Shimanov and Karelin were active in Orthodox dissenting circles in the 1960s – and that Shimanov was interned in a mental ward for his outspoken religious beliefs – it seems odd that they should have arrived at their present position. Two related factors seem to have prompted this change of orientation: a radical disillusionment with the programs of Soviet dissidents who look to the West (the *demokraty*) for Russia's future and an increasing belief that the West, and especially the United States of America, represents the true spiritual danger for contemporary Russia.

Shimanov, who, one presumes, has never been to the United States, sets himself up as a specialist in the politics and mores of that alien land. He admits that, for the untutored Russian mind, the United States can appear quite attractive. "Freedom and riches! . . . What more, it would seem, does a man need in life?"[149] But, as Shimanov seeks to demonstrate at length, the United States is a deadly siren; her vaunted "freedom" is a deceptive mirage. In reality, a "secret dictatorship of capital" rules the country, largely through its control over the mass media, and her vaunted elections represent a complete fraud.[150] The Republican and Democratic parties are both "gigantic parties of big business."[151] A strict and exceedingly "cunning" censorship effectively throttles all dissenting views. In sum, the United States "does not give man true freedom. . . . "[152] (Many of Shimanov's views go back to Lenin.)

For Shimanov, the United States today indicates the direction being taken by all of Western civilization; even the Soviet Union is in danger of being enticed by its example. Due to the expert deception with which the United States masks its true essence, it is able to entrap numerous other societies in the world: ". . . . have not these American gifts already brought the whole world to a global crisis?"[153] Shimanov and his coauthors recoil before this latter-day Babylon with its "disintegration of natural ties, moral vacuum, alienation, terror and consumer attitude toward one's neighbors."[154] ". . . . Western civilization," Shimanov proclaims, "has indeed rotted, because are not all these psychedelic and sexual revolutions, doors covered with armor against robbers, social storms, and the devouring spirit of mercantilism – are they not moral rot?"[155] It is only fair to note that Shimanov nevertheless believes that people still exist in the West with "a love for the good."[156]

The *Mnogaia leta* contributors maintain that the United States is especially dangerous for a Christian. While no one is *openly* persecuted for his faith, "everything that is religious is wiped out. . . . "[157] "Religion dies under the onslaught of a godless style of life."[158] Moreover, in the United States "pan-legal ideology" steps forth as a "veiled super-religion."[159] This situation is obviously more dangerous for a believer than the open atheism promulgated in Soviet society. And it is something that the Western-oriented democrats, who bear "the imprint of a specifically American spirit," fail to see.[160]

The United States and the West are not merely "rotting"; they are also victims of a fearful conspiracy, one of whose principal aims is to catch Russia in its grasp. This plot, which may be termed the "Jewish-Masonic-Plutocratic" conspiracy, has, of course, had a long and notorious history in both the West and Russia. One finds a belief in it in circulation in France at the time of the Dreyfus affair (where it was known as the "Jewish-Masonic-Protestant" conspiracy), and it was imported into Russia some time in the nineteenth century. Being religious men, the *Mnogaia leta* contributors seek to give the theory an appropriately religious explanation. The author of this monstrous conspiracy, they believe, is neither a Jew, nor a Mason, nor a plutocrat, but the devil himself. The conspiracy is intimately connected with the coming rule of Antichrist, as foretold in the scriptures. Yet, despite the acute peril represented by this conspiracy, the authors feel that Russia will find the wisdom and strength to withstand it.

Concerning the Jewish component of the conspiracy, Shimanov and his coauthors repeatedly insist that they are not anti-Semites. ". . . . there is *no* anti-Semitism in Orthodoxy," the anonymous author of "Letter to Fr. Aleksandr Men'" maintains to his readers.[161] The problem is not Jews, who have many positive traits as a people, but Judaism without Christ and, especially, Zionism. "Why does Judaism deceive the Jewish people?" the author of the letter to Fr. Men' asks. "Because for the devil it is especially important to turn precisely the Jewish . . . people (and, through it, as many other peoples as possible) away from the true God. . . . [162] And he continues: ". . . . the most important task of Zionism and of the various organizations inspired by it, such as Masonry and other 'secret' and open societies, is to bring the

Jewish people and as much of humanity as possible under the power of the Antichrist, who will rule in Israel as the 'Messiah'."[163] ". . . . the Antichrist," Felix Karelin asserts, "must come through Judaism."[164]

Intimately linked with Judaism-Zionism in the *Mnogaia leta* conception are Freemasonry and the Western plutocrats. Vladimir Ibragimov seeks to show in his "Anatomy of a Great Mystification" that this unholy alliance made a serious attempt to seize power in Russia during the period 1915–1917. The Masons and Jews were behind Rasputin and the "great mystification," which, as it were, "undermined the Russian monarchy from within."[165] The Masons were highly active during the Duma period and in the February revolution. Oddly, the same Masons who supported Rasputin seemed to have arranged his murder. (Felix Iusupov, who organized the plot, was "a probable participant in a Masonic club.")[166] Nevertheless, "it was not given to the forces of evil to cast a spell on history,"[167] at least not in 1917.

One glaring contradiction is immediately apparent in the historical schema of the *Mnogaia leta* authors. "The Communist revolution," Karelin asserts, "freed Russia, and with it the whole world, from a great danger."[168] So be it. (We will ignore, for the moment, the 25 to 60 million victims of the Stalin terror.) But if that is the case, why do the almanac's contributors write so disparagingly of the early period of Soviet power? "It would be good," Shimanov advises, "if the Jews were to recognize the international character of the Russian revolution. . . . "[169] Many of the early Soviet leaders and concentration camp chieftains were Jews and other non-Russians; Djugashvili-Stalin was, of course, a Georgian.[170] How, one wonders, could an internationalist clique, heavily infiltrated by Jews, save Russia from the Jewish-Masonic conspiracy? Indeed, how do we know that Trotskii and Stalin were not Masons? There is a glaring lapse in the almanac's logic at this point.

As for the third component of the conspiracy, the plutocrats, they are believed to control the United States and much of the West through their stranglehold on the mass media.

"The combination of apparent freedom and secret dependence [on the plutocrats]," Shimanov muses, "what could be simpler and more ingenious?"[171] In an ambitious essay, Felix Karelin attempts to explain the emergence of the plutocrats with reference to eucharistic theology. "The tendency of one or another people," he writes, "to participate in capitalist development was in strict reverse proportion to its participation in the Eucharistic Meal."[172] Thus there is a direct connection between absence of holy communion and capitalism. It is noteworthy, he believes, that Judaism has flourished "in those countries in which Calvinism realized its greatest victories: in the Netherlands, England, and, finally, America."[173] In 1917, Russian liberalism made an attempt to turn Russia "into a demi-colony of Western capital,"[174] but failed.

Such then is the vast conspiracy, directed by the devil, which seeks to draw Russia into its clutches. It is understandable that the *Mnogaia leta* authors should seek to move closer to the Soviet authorities, whose bayonets protect them from Lucifer's legions. Essentially, they argue for a concordat between Orthodox Christians and the Soviet state.

The ideological and theological framework for this concordat is advanced by Karelin in his essay "Two Testimonies." Perhaps influenced by the writings of the "Red Dean" of Canterbury and other Western apologists for the Soviet regime, he points to the property held in common by the early Christians (described in Acts, chapters 2 and 4) and to Christian monasticism as examples of "Christian communism."[175] It was the Christian empire created by Constantine the Great that brought about "the class structure of society" and of Christian government.[176] In Russia, this false "Byzantine" model of social relations gained strength from the end of the fifteenth century and continued through to the reign of Nicholas II.[177] The Bolshevik Revolution, which happily brought the "Constantine period" to an end, was terribly misunderstood by the participants in the Russian Church Council of 1917–1918 and is still misunderstood by many Orthodox Christians today (especially by the Russian Orthodox Church in Exile, an émigré ecclesiastical organization). Rather than ushering in the age of the Antichrist, the revolution provided a new, promising setting for the working of divine providence. Patriarch Tikhon, the first Russian patriarch of the Soviet period (and the first since the reign of Peter the Great) began to see the situation correctly in 1919, after an initial period of sharp opposition to the Bolsheviks.

For Karelin, as for the other *Mnogaia leta* contributors, Tikhon represents a kind of church father on the question of church-state relations; they fully approve of his supposed "historiosophical position."[178] Karelin writes: " . . . Patriarch Tikhon (for the first time on Orthodox soil!) repudiated the principle of old Christian government. . . . "[179] Patriarch Tikhon, he continues, "was inspired from above: the Russian Revolution was indeed neither a temporary time of troubles (*smuta*) nor the advent of the Antichrist."[180] For the edification of his religious readers, Karelin points to various signs confirming the truth of his views. Thus Tikhon's fateful reorientation occurred on October 8, 1919, the day the Russian Church commemorates St. Sergius of Radonezh and the eve of the feast of St. John the Divine. Karelin also makes much of the Roman Catholic miracle of Fatima and its alleged significance for Russia.

The anonymous author of "To Sergei I . . . v" argues for a concordat in a somewhat different vein. "In general," he writes, "I would like to proclaim something like an apology for our Soviet pashas. No, I have never felt love for them, nor do I now. But all of them are our people, our species (*nasha poroda*), the same flesh and bone as you and I. They are simply more unfortunate than we, having become enmeshed in ideological nets. . . . They are our Russian people, not at all stupid and not at all evil. . . . "[181] Compared to the forces at work in the contemporary West, the Soviet ruling elite does not look at all bad: "If you should chance to have a frank conversation with them, they will tell you that everything is bad in our country, that you will scarcely be able to build communism with such a people, but, in response to your liberal hints, they will explain that one cannot let the people get out of hand, that if that were to happen, such things would occur as could not be foreseen even in a nightmare. . . .[182] (The Grand Inquisitor syndrome!) There is a need, such Soviet "pashas" insist, for "party control." The author of "To Sergei I . . . v" is clearly sympathetic to this expressed fear of anarchy and belief in discipline and control; only the excessive attention to ideology needs to be mitigated.

The rule of the Bolsheviks, the *Mnogaia leta* authors conclude, has been God's will. "Despite the prognoses of the [1917–1918] Church Council," Karelin writes, "the Russian atheist state has been standing on earth almost 63 years . . . "[183] Shimanov believes that, in historical perspective, the October Revolution "did not produce only negative results; the positive results outweigh the negative ones by a great deal."[184] "I understand," Ibragimov responds to charges by émigré writer Andrei Siniavskii, "that you are against the cooperation of the church and the Soviet government. But what if, against your expectations, this cooperation should turn out for the good?"[185]

Mnogaia leta thus offers a critique of the contemporary West and a defense of the proposition that Orthodox believers and the Soviet regime should cooperate. Does it also elaborate a positive program for the direction Soviet society should be taking in the coming decades? A loosely articulated program of this sort is advocated by the almanac's authors. The general secularization of the world, Karelin writes, "is perhaps ending before our eyes."[186] And in his essay "Primal Sources and Roots," A. Kazakov sees a "birth of new ideologies" occurring throughout the world.[187] It is, however, largely left to Shimanov, in his quasi-programmatic "To Leah Abramson," to suggest what the future Russia might look like.

The false secular models of the West, Shimanov argues here, must be replaced by a "religio-patriarchal organization of life," one that, however, does not ignore the discoveries and advances of modern technology. Shimanov does not desire a pastoralization of the USSR. He is opposed to an "ossification or even primitivization of scientific and technical, social, and cultural possibilities, a halt to development, a repudiation of creativity."[188]

Shimanov is particularly interested in the volatile "nationalities question" in the USSR. "The new type of free association (*soobshchestvo*)" he advocates is one in which "the sovereignty of each small nation over its territory would be recognized by the large nation and fortified by the right of each nation to leave the association – a right not subject to discussion [by the large nation]. . . . "[189] Jews disillusioned with Zionism would be offered land somewhere in the USSR – elsewhere Shimanov has suggested the Crimea as an appropriate location – in order to form their own nation-state. In free association with ethnic Russians, the peoples of the USSR and Eastern Europe would enjoy national security and the right to linguistic and cultural freedom.[190] Because practically a majority of present-day Russians are the product of mixed marriages with neighboring peoples, that is are related to these peoples by blood, there would be an added incentive for such associations.[191]

This necessarily sketchy outline of the central ideas presented in *Mnogaia leta* is sufficient to suggest the reasons for the tolerance the Brezhnev regime demonstrated toward the almanac. The authors' radical hostility toward the contemporary West could not but have proved welcome, as must their commitment to cooperation between Orthodox Christians and the Soviet state; and their enmity toward dissident Soviet democrats must also have been appreciated. On the other hand, other elements in the almanac's repertoire would have been less welcome: for example, its emphasis on the "alien" character of early Soviet power (which, according to this interpretation, extended through the reign of Stalin!), its sporadic and muted but nevertheless noticeable criticism of antireligious persecution, its commitment to a belief in the Jewish-Masonic-Plutocratic conspiracy, which, while a useful substitute for Marxist-Leninist ideology, does not mesh particularly well with it. Some of the marginal contributions to the almanac could have been seen as expressing borderline sentiments. "Terrible is the world of atheistic ideology," writes V. Trostnikov, "in which we live."[192] And Tat'iana Chernysheva criticizes contemporary Soviet architecture for its hideous multistorey edifices and notes the "beheading" and ruination of Russian churches that took place in the recent past."[193] One also doubts whether the Soviet authorities would approve *Mnogaia leta's* liberal stance on the nationalities question.

I now come to my own criticism of the almanac. It is, frankly, difficult to know where to begin. (Indeed *Mnogaia leta* will undoubtedly appear so extreme to many readers that they may wonder why I took the time to review it at all. I will attempt to deal with this question later.) The views of Shimanov and his associates on the contemporary West are in large part due to Soviet blockage of information and to the inability of Soviet citizens to travel abroad. I am not claiming that if they were able to spend considerable time in the West they would necessarily become enthusiasts. Solzhenitsyn, whose views on certain questions bear a resemblance to those of the *Mnogaia leta* authors, has been in the West for some time and has been critical of much that he has seen. But Solzhenitsyn realizes that the West is not in thrall to a Jewish-Masonic-Plutocratic conspiracy; rather, he sees the West as in danger of falling into a policy of appeasement before the expansionist threat represented by the USSR and its materialistic and atheistic ideology. (Solzhenitsyn would also reject with repugnance any suggestion of the need for a concordat between Orthodox Christians and the Soviet state.) One suspects that the almanac's authors' incredibly distorted and caricatured view of how the West functions *would* change if they could visit the West. They would learn, for example, that elections frequently do mean something and that not all media are uniformly controlled by plutocrats. Needless to say, the "not at all evil" bosses of the USSR are unlikely to let the *Mnogaia leta* contributors come to the West to see for themselves.

Along with their obsessive conspiracy theory, the authors' most dubious point is their advocacy of a close cooperation between the Soviet state and Russian Orthodox Christians. "By their fruits ye shall know them." What have been the fruits of the Bolshevik regime over the past 65 years? Some Sputniks, some giant hydroelectric stations, a formidable military machine, to be sure. But also a holocaust exceeding Hitler's in the number of victims; the Gulag Archipelago; a country rent by alcoholism, growing infant mortality, and juvenile delinquency. To claim that the pathetically weak Masons of the February Revolution represented a greater danger to the country than did the Bolsheviks is simply absurd. It was the Bolsheviks who launched the severest persecution in the history of the Orthodox Church, a persecution that continues today, as scores of documents sent to the West by the recently surpassed Christian Committee for the Defense of Believers' Rights in the USSR confirm. The most recently revised Soviet legislation on religion also testifies to this.[194]

The attempt to turn Patriarch Tikhon into a "church father" in the area of church-state relations is both dishonest and deceiving. If Tikhon had chosen to bless the White Army in 1919, he would have been immediately arrested and a hireling put in his place. Furthermore, like Aleksandr Nevskii, he found himself fighting a war on two fronts: against the Bolsheviks on the one hand and the Renovationists (a dangerous schism and heresy) on the other. This important fact is ignored by Karelin, though he does in one place admit to a distaste for the Renovationists. Simply put, Marxism-Leninism and Orthodoxy are not compatible: Lenin and Trotskii realized this clearly; Kuroedev, head of the Council for Religious Affairs from 1960–1985, realized it; and so should Karelin.

In a few areas, the *Mnogaia leta* authors deserve to be complimented. It was good to see that they reject Stalin and his deeds (not all right wing nationalists do), and their suggested solution to the nationalities question in the USSR, although utopian, is not mean spirited. If, as they claim, Shimanov and his associates truly wish to attract others, including people in the West, through superior ethical behavior, I for one would have no objection. They might begin by agitating for the withdrawal of Soviet troops from Afghanistan.

I have promised to explain why an almanac as extreme as *Mnogaia leta* deserves any attention in these pages. First of all, most programs coming out of the present-day Soviet

Union are likely to be extreme. After 65 years of totalitarian rule, the USSR is in many ways a very sick country. Class war, genocide, breakneck industrialization – all have taken a heavy spiritual toll. Konrad Adenauer, seeking to explain the rise of national socialism in Germany, wrote in his memoirs:

> The rapid increase in industrialization, the concentration of large masses of people in the cities, and, a connected phenomenon, the uprooting of many people, cleared the way for the pernicious growth of materialism among the German people. A materialist ideology was bound further to emphasize the importance of power and of the State which gathered and embodied this power, and to lead to the subordination of ethical values and of the dignity of the individual.
>
> Marxist materialism contributed a great deal to this development. Anyone who works for the centralization of political and economic power in the hands of the State or of one class, and who therefore advocates the principle of class war, is an enemy of freedom of the individual and is bound to prepare the way for dictatorship in the minds of his adherents. . . .[195]

I am not saying that Shimanov and his friends are National Socialists. Their sincere, if at times bizarre, religious convictions distinguish them from the neopagan Nazis. Their views, however, bear a certain undeniable resemblance to fascism, as I shall show later in this chapter. As Adenauer maintains, Marxist materialism can easily generate a right wing extremism. The Jewish-Masonic-Plutocratic conspiracy, to take one example, feeds on the Marxist legacy of class suspicions, dark paranoias, and conspiracy theories. One wonders whether it is an accident that Shimanov is the son of former activists in the League of Militant Godless.

Now for some comments on the underlying religious problems of the *Mnogaia leta* authors. Felix Karelin is wrong: what occurred in the late fifteenth century was not an adoption of Byzantinism by the Muscovite State but rather a decisive rejection of the Greek patristic synthesis and the spiritual method of hesychasm by the orientation known as "Josephitism" (*Iosiflianstvo*, named after Joseph of Volotsk [Volokolamsk]). The Greek patristic synthesis and hesychasm, simply put, *are* Orthodox Christianity in its purity and intellectual-spiritual depth.[196] When Joseph and his followers defeated Nil Sorskii and the so-called Trans-Volgan elders, a period of religious decline set in that eventually culminated in the tragic Old Believer schism (*raskol*) of the late seventeenth century. That tragedy, in turn, made Peter the Great's secularization of the Russian church possible. In the late eighteenth–early nineteenth centuries, there was a hesychast revival in Russia through the efforts of *Starets* Paisii Velichkovskii, who had been to Mount Athos. The most famous representatives of this movement were the *startsy* of Optina Pustyn' Monastery, who attracted Nikolai Gogol', Dostoevskii, Tolstoi, Ivan Kireevskii, Vladimir Solov'ev, Konstantin Leont'ev, and numerous other intellectuals.

The Bolshevik Revolution suppressed this remarkable spiritual-intellectual renaissance, and Optina Pustyn' now lies in ruins, though Vladimir Soloukhin has been attempting to dramatize its plight.[197] When deprived of the wisdom, balance, and sobriety of hesychasm, the Russian religious mind inevitably sinks into Josephitism. Dostoevskii, for one, was quite aware of this – one thinks of the demon-ridden Ferapont, opponent of *Starets* Zosima in *The Brothers Karamazov*, or of the charlatan Semen Iakovlevich in *The Devils*, or of the various aberrant Old Believers, Flagellants, and Castrates whose shadows darken his great novels. Dostoevskii believed that not only the atheistic-socialist West threatened Russia, but also a primitive, earthbound indigenous religiosity, unillumined by the catholic mind of the Orthodox Church. One should note that Josephites are traditionally transfixed by "signs" and gaudy "miracles," that they place an extreme emphasis on the devil, whose workings they proudly claim to understand fully, and that they maintain an external, rigorous piety.

Cut off from the sources of pure Orthodoxy by the Soviet suppression of information and affected by the illnesses of

Soviet society, the *Mnogaia leta* authors represent a clear-cut neo-Josephite tendency. It strikes one as no accident that Shimanov chooses to append a short story devoted to a courageous but ignorant Old Believer woman to the 1981 almanac.[198] Karelin and Ibragimov are haunted by various signs and wonders. Interestingly, Ibragimov indicts the court of Nicholas II for having become enmeshed "in a labyrinth of prophecies."[199] That is true, but the authors of *Mnogaia leta* are just as enmeshed. Missing are sobriety, discernment, "the testing of thoughts," self-discipline, and mental and spiritual rigor. They claim to read the Apocalypse as an open book. The Optina *startsy* would undoubtedly indict them for *prelest'* (spiritual deceit).

The almanac's contributors also betray the influence of Marxist determinism in their attitude toward the Bolshevik regime. Because it has been around for more than 60 years, they argue, its existence must be God's will. But such an affirmation ignores an elementary theological distinction between what God *permits* and what he *wills* to happen. Christ permitted Judas to betray him, but it would have been better had Judas not been born.

A final task in this chapter will be to attempt to place the *Mnogaia leta* collections within the present-day Russian nationalist spectrum.*

The two most significant Russian nationalist tendencies today are what Solzhenitsyn has termed "the Russian national and religious renaissance,"[200] whose adherents I shall call *vozrozhdentsy*, after the Russian word for renaissance, and the tendency usually known as National Bolshevism.

Virtually all dissenting nationalists – Solzhenitsyn, Igor' Shafarevich, Osipov, Igor' Ogurtsov – can be counted among the ranks of *vozrozhdentsy*, as can perhaps a majority of so-called ruralist writers whose quasi-Aesopian works appear

---

*The following is a condensed version of a chapter from the author's book, *The Faces of Contemporary Russian Nationalism* (Princeton: Princeton University Press, 1983).

in Soviet literary journals: Valentin Rasputin, Vasili Belov, and the late Fedor Abramov. Figures such as nationalist painter Il'ia Glazunov can impressionistically be seen as straddling the fence separating *vozrozhdentsy* from National Bolsheviks. Programmatic efforts of the *vozrozhdenets* tendency are the VSKhSON "Program" (1964), Solzhenitsyn's *Letter to the Soviet Leaders* (1974), the collection *From Under the Rubble* (1974), and the "Declaration of Principles" of the Moscow Religio-Philosophical Seminar (1978). Most *vozrozhdentsy* would agree on the following: the need to jettison Marxism-Leninism as the state ideology; the need for economic and administrative decentralization; the necessity of building up the church, family, and school (without, however, reestablishing the Russian church); decollectivization of agriculture and the introduction of a mixed economy; an emphasis on internal development; and withdrawal from involvement in the affairs of other nations. Issues on which there would be less agreement are the degree of authority that the state or head of state should enjoy, the manner in which accommodation should be reached with the minority nationalities of the USSR, and the degree to which Russia should have economic ties with the West. A significant proportion of *vozrozhdentsy*, interestingly, favor a return to a monarchistic system of government.

Russian Orthodoxy occupies a central position in the thought of *vozrozhdentsy* and serves to insulate them against any accommodation with the "Communist experiment" or with the intensely antireligious founder of the Soviet state, Vladimir Lenin. As for relations with the West, though many find the West distasteful on moral and aesthetic grounds, their antipathy is generally a restrained one.

National Bolshevism, the second important nationalist strand, is a more elusive tendency of thought and sentiment that currently enjoys popularity among certain segments of the Soviet intelligentsia and ruling party-state *apparat*. (If Evgenii Vagin is correct – and I believe he is – National Bolshevism completely lacks a mass base.[201]) A number of official nationalists, such as many ruralist writers, are actually "closet" *vozrozhdentsy* rather than National Bolsheviks.

The term National Bolshevism was coined in 1921 by Nikolai Ustrialov, an émigré professor living in Harbin, China and the most influential contributor to the *Smena vekh* (Change of Landmarks) collection. The *smenovekhovtsy* advocated a rapprochement between the Bolshevik Revolution and the Russian state, to be achieved through a squeezing out of the "internationalist" elements of the revolution. The original National Bolsheviks were not religious, but neither were they hostile to religion, and, while opposed to a restoration of monarchy, they argued for the need for a strong dictatorship. The similarities between National Bolshevism and fascism are striking: a strong impulse toward deification of the nation; the desire for a strong state, the *stato totalitario*; a powerful leadership impulse (one thinks of the yearning among many contemporary National Bolsheviks for a "strong man" [*krepkii chelovek*]); a belief in the necessity of an elite; a cult of discipline, particularly of the youth; heroic vitalism; an acceptance of military and industrial might, often combined with strong ecological and preservationist concerns; and a celebration of the glories of the past.

Sergei Semanov's collection of essays *Serdtse rodiny* (Heart of the Homeland, 1977) represents a useful compendium of National Bolshevik concerns.[202] In his book, Semanov focuses on the need for and benefits accruing from Soviet Russian patriotism. He promotes a "single stream" interpretation of Russian history, simultaneously lauding Aleksandr Suvorov and Mikhail Kutuzov, Mikhail Frunze and Georgii Zhukov. Like one of his avowed mentors, the writer Aleksei N. Tolstoi, Semanov attempts to combine patriotic and Communist motifs in his writings, although Marxist ideological elements are less evident than in Tolstoi, while nationalist (and even Russian Orthodox) elements receive heightened emphasis. Semanov believes (though he expresses the conviction somewhat cautiously) in a Jewish-Masonic conspiracy and sees the Russophobic West as essentially controlled by "international Masonic and Zionist financial circles."[203]

Other recent works of National Bolshevik inspiration are

Nikolai Iakovlev's *1 August 1914*, published by *Molodaia gvardiia* in 1974 in an edition of 100 thousand copies, and Valentin Pikul's controversial novel *U poslednei cherty* (At the Last Frontier), which appeared in *Nash sovremennik* during 1979.[204] National Bolsheviks like to deal with historical topics, particularly the period immediately preceding or following the Bolshevik Revolution – this allows them to speak to the present using political examples from the past. Implementation of the ideas of the National Bolsheviks would probably lead to what Alain Besançon calls "a pan-Russian police and military empire."[205]

As should be evident, National Bolsheviks and *vozrozhdentsy* share a number of concerns and attitudes, and it is this area of common interest that allows one to view both as being in some fashion "Russian nationalist." Both tendencies are preservationist, seeking to safeguard Russian historical monuments and the Russian environment from defilement and destruction; both deplore present demographic and social trends as unfavorable to the well-being of the Russian people; both are "polycentric" nationalists, desiring, at least in words, the cultural flourishing of all nationalities in the USSR and elsewhere. In addition, both tendencies exhibit a keen interest in Russian conservative and patriotic thought of the past. The crucial difference between the two tendencies lies in their attitude toward Russian Orthodoxy and in their willingness to achieve at least a temporary modus vivendi with Marxism-Leninism.

Orthodoxy represents the pivot of the thought of most *vozrozhdentsy*, while National Bolsheviks lean toward a quasi-deification of the Russian people. In the eyes of *vozrozhdentsy*, there can be no accommodation with atheistic, internationalist, Russophobic, antivillage Marxism-Leninism; National Bolsheviks, on the other hand, are willing to make tactical compromises with it. Other differences between the two tendencies center on the question of military-industrial might and urban growth – which National Bolsheviks would not necessarily oppose, in spite of considerable ecological and preservationist sentiment – and on the wisdom of conducting an aggressive foreign policy. At times, *vozrozhdentsy* and National Bolsheviks clash – such a difference of opinion seems to have been at least partly behind the 1973–1974 split of *Veche* editors and authors into two opposing camps – but the two tendencies are often able to recognize a certain communality of interest.

As far as the strength of the two tendencies is concerned, the *vozrozhdentsy* would appear to have the numbers, while the National Bolsheviks might be better positioned actually to assume power. If the National Bolsheviks were to come to power, they would undoubtedly be more receptive to the arguments of the intellectually sophisticated *vozrozhdentsy*, with whom they have ideational and emotional links, than are the present Soviet leaders. A possible development therefore, might be a brief National Bolshevik interregnum separating Marxist-Leninist and *vozrozhdenets* periods of rule. The most likely vehicle for a National Bolshevik accession to power would be the Soviet military.[206]

It should be clear that the almanac *Mnogaia leta* straddles the line dividing what we have termed *vozrozhdentsy* from National Bolsheviks. In their sincere, though often misguided, religiosity, its authors represent the *vozrozhdenets* tendency; in their fixation with the Jewish-Masonic-Plutocratic conspiracy and in their extreme hostility toward the West, they resemble the National Bolsheviks. This equivocation may well be intentional on the part of the *Mnogaia leta* authors; they are making overtures to the National Bolsheviks, seeking an understanding that would find a place for Russian Orthodoxy in Soviet society. But such a compromise cannot bear good fruit. The *vozrozhdenets* tendency, with its uncompromising opposition to Marxist-Leninist ideology and its nobility of vision and purpose, offers the only viable Russian nationalist way out of the morass in which the Soviet Union presently finds itself.

Notes

1. For this figure, see *Sel'skaia zhizn'*, May 17, 1984, p. 2.

2. For this figure, see *Izvestiia*, December 11, 1982, p. 2.

3. For this figure, see my *The Faces of Contemporary Russian Nationalism* (Princeton, N.J.: Princeton University Press, 1983), 169–170, note 9.

4. Martin Malia, *Comprendre la Révolution Russe* (Paris: Editions du Seuil, 1980), 223. Malia concludes his series of lectures with these words concerning the Soviet system: "A l'intérieur, le système est incapable de se réformer, de se libéraliser, de se 'social-démocratiser,' parce que les seules reformes nécessaires liquideraient le système lui-même. La solution est à l'extérieur: le régime est voué à l'expansion, une expansion qui, en réalité, n'est qu'une fuite en avant." (p. 227)

Malia appears to have been influenced by the thought of Leszek Kolakowski. See, in particular, Kolakowski's magisterial three-volume study, *Main Currents of Marxism* (Oxford: Clarendon Press, 1978). Carl Linden is another scholar who has arrived at conclusions similar to those of Malia. See his *The Soviet Party-State: The Politics of Ideocratic Despotism* (New York: Praeger, 1983).

5. Alain Besançon, *Présent Soviétique et Passé Russe* (Paris: Le Livre de Poche, 1980), 24.

6. In his collection of essays *An Ideology in Power*, Bertram Wolfe correctly notes that Soviet conduct of foreign affairs is "a composite of disparate and conflicting forces, namely: (1) the influence of the traditional situation of the nation upon those who

usurped power there; (2) the alterations forced upon them by recalcitrant reality; and (3) the drives and preconceptions of the intensely held ideology which they possess, and which possesses them." Bertram Wolfe, *An Ideology in Power* (New York: Stein and Day, 1969), 346. It is of course Wolfe's third point that distinguishes Soviet foreign policy from that of the tsars.

7. On this, see my forthcoming essay "Language, Culture, Religion and National Awareness" which will appear in Robert Conquest, ed., *The Last Empire*, a volume to be published in 1985 by the Hoover Institution Press.

8. Because Russian serves as the *lingua franca* of the Soviet Union, the broadcasting situation is necessarily complex. The obvious solution is to find a proper mix of programs aimed at ethnic Russians and those geared to all Russian-speaking Soviet citizens.

9. See the interview with Besançon entitled "La Technique du Pouvoir en URSS," *L'Express*, December 2–9, 1978, p. 92.

10. On the *Molodaia gvardiia* episode, see Dunlop, *The Faces of Contemporary Russian Nationalism*, 39–44, 216–227.

11. Vladimir Shubkin, "Neopalimaia kupina," *Nash sovremennik* 12 (1981): 175–188.

12. R. Gal'tseva and I. Rodnianskaia, "'Brat'ia Karamazovy' kak nravstvennyi zavet Dostoevskogo," *Sever* 8, (1981): 102–109.

13. Anatolii Znamenskii, "Pravda zhizni – pravda isskustva," *Sever* 2, (1981): 118–122.

14. Vadim Kozhinov, "I nazovet menia vsiak sushchii v nei iazyk . . . ," *Nash sovremennik* 11, (1981): 153–176. (For a detailed discussion of National Bolshevism, see the concluding section of the final essay in this collection.)

15. On this, see Roy Medvedev, "The Death of the 'Chief Ideologue,'" *New Left Review* (November–December 1982); and Semen Reznik, "Kto takoi Sergei Semanov?" *Novaia gazeta* (New York), December 11–17, 1982. An American who was a frequent visitor to Il'ia Glazunov's workshop in the late 1970s provided me with the same information.

16. The volume *Khudozhnik i Rossiia* (Dusseldorf: "Grad Kitezh," 1980) contains the comment books for the Moscow and Leningrad exhibits.

17. On this almanac, see chapter 7.

18. Medvedev, "The Death of the 'Chief Ideologue,'" 56.

19. Klaus Mehnert, *The Russians and Their Favorite Books* (Stanford, Calif.: Hoover Institution Press, 1983).

20. See Iurii Surovtsev, "Polemicheskie marginalii," *Znamia* 9 (1981): 222–223; and Z. Tazhurizina and K. Nikonov, "Chto takoe starchestvo," *Nauka i religiia* 4 (1981): 38; 5 (1981): 24; 6 (1981): 34 and 36.

21. "Pochta zhurnala," *Kommunist* 2 (1982): 127–128 (this issue went to print on January 25, 1982); and V. Kuleshov, "Tochnost' kriteriev," *Pravda*, February 1, 1982, p. 7. For a discussion of the attacks on the Russian nationalists in the period following Suslov's death, see Mark Higgie, "From Brezhnev to Andropov," *Soviet Analyst* (August 3, 1983):6–8 and (August 17, 1983): 6–8.

22. On these arrests, see "Khronika," *Posev* 11 (1982): 3; "Chto proiskhodit v strane: Rasskazyvaet Georgii Vladimov," *Posev* 7 (1983): 28–29; and "KGB protiv literatury: Rasskazyvaet Georgii Vladimov," *Posev* 8 (1983): 37–39; and Semen Reznik, "Kto takoi Sergei Semanov," 10.

23. Iuliia Voznesenskaia, "Soobshchenie iz kluba 'Maria,'" *Russkaia mysl'* 10 (June 1982): 6.

24. "Delo o religioznom samizdate," *Posev* 6 (1982): 6–7.

25. "Pochta zhurnala," *Kommunist* 8 (1982): 128. This issue went to press on May 19, 1982.

26. Vladimov, "KGB protiv literatury," 39; and Reznik, "Kto takoi Sergei Semanov," 10.

27. Vladimov, "Chto proiskhodit v strane," 27.

28. "V Tsentral'nom Komitete KPSS," *Pravda*, July 30, 1982, p. 1; "Mesto pisatelia v gushche zhizni," *Pravda*, August 5, 1982, p. 1; and "V Tsentral'nom Komitete KPSS," *Literaturnaia gazeta*, August 4, 1982, p. 1. On the decree, see M. Nazarov, "Dostignet li tseli 'literaturnoe' postanovlenie TsK?" *Posev* 12 (1982): 50–55; and Sergei Yurenen, "The Literary Process in the USSR in Light of the Latest Decree," Radio Liberty Research Bulletin, RL 408/82, October 8, 1982.

29. Iu.V. Andropov, "Shest'desiat let SSSR," *Pravda*, December 22, 1982. Andropov's speech also appeared in a booklet edition of 3 million copies, published by Izdatel'stvo politicheskoi literatury in December 1982. For discussions of the relationship of his speech to the "nationalities issue," see Ann Sheehy, "Andropov Speaks on Nationalities Policy," RL 510/82, December 21, 1982; the same author's "Andropov and the Merging of Nations," RL 516/82, December 22, 1982; and Roman Solchanyk, "Merger of Nations: Back in Style?" RL 84/83, February 18, 1983.

30. On this, see S. Enders Wimbush, *Contemporary Russian*

Nationalist Responses to Non-Russians in the USSR, Rand Corporation research paper P-5941, March 1978, passim.

31. Zhores Medvedev, *Andropov* (Oxford, England: Basil Blackwell, 1983), 18.

32. Petr Proskurin, "Slovo zăvetnoe," *Pravda*, December 5, 1982, p. 3.

33. See the account in *Literaturnaia gazeta*, "Vremia trebuet!" January 26, 1983, pp. 1–2. See also Nataliya Gross, "Journal *Sever* Draws Party's Fire," RL 70/83, February 7, 1983.

34. Vladimov, "Chto proiskhodit v strane," 28.

35. Ibid. In a recent statement, Vladimov has elaborated upon his earlier comments on the Soviet military: "Without an organized force, one having weapons in its hands, nothing, I think, will happen [in the Soviet Union]. . . . I consider such a force to be the regular officer corps of the army. It is there that the ideas of the 'Russian Party' are penetrating. One can also predict that Afghanistan will turn out to be an accelerator of this process." (See "Diskussiia po dokladu," *Posev* 11 [1984]: 50.)

36. Vladimir Soloukhin, "Kameshki na ladoni," *Nash sovremennik* 3 (1981); 39. (Iurii Seleznev died in June 1984 at the age of 44. See the warm tribute to him in *Literaturnaia Rossiia*, June 22, 1984, p. 22.)

37. Kozhinov, "I nazovet menia vsiak sushchii v nei iazyk . . . ," *Nash sovremennik* 11 (1981): 153–176.

38. Ibid., 173.

39. Sergei Semanov, "Sovremennoe oblich'e starogo vraga," *Nash sovremennik* 7 (1981): 189.

40. On the issue of preservation, see, for example, the following: Oleg Gusev, "Kak byt' s volkom," 5 (1981); Vladimir Soloukhin, "Rodnaia Tret'iakovka," 5 (1981) and "Prodolzhenie vremeni," 1 (1982); and Al'bert Semin, "Nastalo vremia berezhnogo otnosheniia k mikromiru," 6 (1981).

41. On alcoholism, see, for example: Nikolai Mashovets, "O trezvosti," 6 (1981); Petr Dudochkin, "Trezvost'–norma zhizni," 8 (1981); "Trezvost'–norma zhizni," 11 (1981). On the preservation of the Russian family, see Boris Sporov, "Vzaimosviaz': Sem'ia, brak, razvod," 9 (1981), and O. Soloukhina, "Na chto i klad, koli v sem'e lad," 2 (1982).

42. See, for example, Ivan Vasil'ev, "Zemlia russkaia," 1 (1981) and 12 (1981); Ol'ga Fokina, "Vmeste s rodimym polem," 1 (1981); Svetlana Mart'ianova, "Dereven'ka moia," 1 (1981); N. Novikov,

"Sprashivaet . . . sobstevennaia sovest'," 4 (1981); Anatolii Rogov, "Dom, derevnia, zemlia . . . ," 7 (1981); Dm. Kuzovlev, "Afonin dom," 10 (1981); Leonid Ivanov, "Opiat' ia v derevne," 10 (1981); Ivan Vasil'ev, "Khvala domu moemu," 2 (1982); Vladimir Sitnikov, "Budut svad'by na sele," 3 (1982).

43. Vasilii Belov, "Lad" in nos. 1, 5, 6, and 7 for 1981.

44. On the "Gypsy affair" and the *Avrora* attack, see *New York Times*, March 6, 1982, p. 2.

45. Vladimir Soloukhin, "Prodolzhenie vremeni," *Nash sovremennik* 1 (1982): 18–30.

46. "Pochta zhurnala," *Kommunist* 2 (1982): 127–128.

47. Z. Tazhurzina and N. Nikonov, "Chto takoe starchestvo," *Nauka i religiia* 4 (1981): 38; 5 (1981) 24; 6 (1981) 34 and 36; Iurii Surovtsev, "Polemicheskie marginalii," *Znamia* 9 (1981): 222–223. 222–223.

48. V. Kuleshov, "Tochnost' kriteriev," *Pravda*, February 1, 1982, p. 7.

49. Vladimir Soloukhin, "Kameshki na ladoni," *Nash sovremennik* 3 (1982): 79: "Esli my budem rassmatrivat' liuboi mekhanizm v prirode . . . my ne mozhem ne priiti k odnomu ochen' prostomu vyvodu: produmanno."

50. Apollon Kuz'min, "Pisatel' i istoriia," *Nash sovremennik* 4 (1982): 156–157.

51. "Pochta zhurnala," *Kommunist* 8 (1982): 128.

52. Mikhail S. Bernstam, "Evaluating the Relative Strength of Social Lobbies in the USSR," Unpublished manuscript, August 1984.

53. "V Tsentral'nom Komitete KPSS i Sovete Ministrov SSSR," *Pravda*, May 6, 1984, pp. 1–2.

54. *The Times* (London), May 7, 1984, p. 6.

55. There are indications that Chernenko has attempted to retain the ideological portfolio after becoming general secretary and president. In an interview appearing in the March 15, 1984 issue of *Dagens Nyheter* (Stockholm), *Pravda* editor Viktor Afanas'ev is reported to have said: "'Gorbachev has the same key position in the party that Suslov had. He is now in charge of the work of the Central Committee Secretariat.' However Gorbachev is not a 'chief ideologist,' which is what Suslov was. Chernenko himself sees to ideology." (The interview was summarized in Foreign Broadcast Information Service (*FBIS*), March 22, 1984, p. R1.) While serving as Andropov's party secretary for ideology, Chernenko came

out sharply against the Russian nationalists. See, for example, his major address: "Aktual'nye voprosy ideologicheskoi, massovo-politicheskoi raboty partii," *Pravda*, June 15, 1983. In this speech, Chernenko scored "deviations from historical truth, for example in the evaluation of collectivization, as well as 'God-seeking' motifs, and an idealization of patriarchal-ness" and worried aloud over "the influence of religion" in the USSR. The June plenum and Chernenko's speech are "now regarded as holy writ and constantly referred to as a touchstone of policy." *The Times* (London), May 7, 1984, p. 6.

56. V. Oskotskii, "V bor'be s antiistorizmom," *Pravda*, May 6, 1984, p. 2.

57. On this important episode, see *The Faces of Contemporary Russian Nationalism*, 227–233.

58. S. T. Kaltakhchian, *Marksistsko-leninskaia teoriia natsii i sovremennost'* (Moscow: Izdatel'stvo politicheskoi literatury, 1983).

59. Ibid., 167. On the same page, Kaltakhchian singles out a second article appearing in *Volga* for attack, indicating that the journal is being warned to watch its step in the future. During the Andropov period, the journals *Nash sovremennik* and *Sever* were similarly taken to task.

60. Ibid., 166.

61. Ibid., 168.

62. Ibid., 300.

63. Ibid., 305.

64. For the text of the award, see *Literaturnaia Rossiia*, June 15, 1984, p. 11. That Soloukhin was making a political comeback was evident from a eulogy published the previous month in the journal *Moskva*: Vadim Dement'ev, "Sluzhenie prekrasnomu, K 60-letiiu Vladimira Solukhina," *Moskva* 5 (1984): 192–194.

65. On these developments, see M.N., "Na literaturnom fronte," *Posev* 7 (1984): 4–6; and Sergei Iur'enen, "Vladimir Soloukhin: Reabilitatsiia s voznagrazhdeniem," Radio Liberty Research Paper, RS 133/84, June 26, 1984.

66. Mikhail Bernstam, "Evaluating the Relative Strength . . . "

67. See Sergei Yurenen, "Chernenko's 'Literary' Policy and the Reality of Literature," Radio Liberty Research Paper, RL 371/84, September 28, 1984. For the text of Chernenko's address, see *Pravda*, September 26, 1984, pp. 1–2.

68. See "Ukaz Prezidiuma Verkhovnogo Soveta SSSR," *Literaturnaia gazeta*, November 21, 1984, p. 2.

69. Alain Besançon, "Nationalism and Bolshevism in the USSR." My italics. This essay will be published by the Hoover Institution Press in 1985 as part of a collection of conference papers edited by Robert Conquest. The volume's title will be *The Last Empire*.

70. Ibid.

71. "Ideologiia v razvalinakh" (Interview with eight new émigré writers), *Novaia gazeta* (New York), May 22–28, 1982, p. 5.

72. Stephen White, *Political Culture and Soviet Politics* (London: Macmillan, 1979), 113–142.

73. Alexander Shtromas, "To Fight Communism: Why and How?" Unpublished manuscript, dated December 21, 1983.

74. White, *Political Culture . . .* , p. 140.

75. Besançon, "Nationalism and Bolshevism."

76. Victor Zaslavsky and Robert J. Brym, *Soviet-Jewish Emigration and Soviet Nationality Policy* (London: Macmillan, 1983), 112.

77. Alexander Shtromas, *Political Change and Social Development: The Case of the Soviet Union* (Frankfurt-am-Main: Peter Lang, 1981), 81.

78. See Alexander Yanov, *Detente after Brezhnev* (Berkeley, Calif.: Institute of International Studies, 1977), and *The Russian New Right* (Berkeley, Calif.: Institute of International Studies, 1978).

79. See Shtromas' illuminating discussion of "authoritarianism" in *Political Change and Social Development*, 109–122.

80. Chalmers Johnson, *Revolutionary Change* (Stanford, Calif.: Stanford University Press, 1982), 31.

81. Crane Brinton, *The Anatomy of Revolution* (New York: Vintage, 1965), 234. This volume is a revised and expanded version of a book that was first published in 1938.

82. See Dunlop, *The Faces of Contemporary Russian Nationalism*, 149–154.

83. Ibid., 152.

84. Ibid., 150.

85. Zaslavskii and Brym, *Soviet-Jewish Emigration*, 77–117.

86. Ibid., 112.

87. Ibid., 115.

88. Simon Markish, "Jewish Images in Solzhenitsyn," *Soviet Jewish Affairs* 7, no. 1 (1977): 78–80.

89. Brinton, *The Anatomy of Revolution*, 226–227.

90. Shtromas, *Political Change and Social Development: The Case of the Soviet Union*, 137.

91. M. Kasvinov, "Dvadtsat' tri stupeni vniz" in *Zvezda*, nos. 8 and 9 (1971); 140–176 and 117–172, and Nos. 7, 8, 9, and 10 (1973): 110–152, 113–153, 124–152, and 170–193.

92. M.K. Kasvinov, *Dvadtsat' tri stupeni vniz* (Moscow: "Mysl'," 1979).

93. Ibid., 21.

94. Ibid., 112.

95. Ibid., 523.

96. Ibid., 536.

97. Ibid., 289.

98. See Valentin Pikul', "U poslednei cherty. Roman-khronika" in *Nash sovremennik* 4, 5, 6, and 7 (1979): 19–152, 62–145, 79–120, and 34–127. Pikul' is an anti-monarchist fascist and a believer in the "Jewish-Masonic conspiracy." On this controversial novel, see I. Shenfel'd, "Sovetskaia kniga o Rasputine," *Russkaia mysl'*, September 20, 1979, p. 7 and September 27, p. 7.

99. See N. Iakovlev, *1 avgusta 1914* (Moscow, *Molodaia gvardiia*, 1974). On Iakovlev, see Vladimir Toltz, "Foremost Soviet Historian Nikolai Yakovlev: A Doughty Opponent of the CIA, Dissidents, and Masons," Radio Liberty Research Paper, RL 386/83, October 17, 1983.

100. See the latest "knot" of Solzhenitsyn's multivolume historical novel on the Russian Revolution: Aleksandr Solzhenitsyn, *Sobranie sochinenii* 12 (Vermont/Paris: YMCA-Press, 1983).

101. See Andrei Amalrik, *Raspoutine* (Paris: Seuil, 1982). The Russian original of this unfinished study has yet to appear in print.

102. On the *Avrora* episode, see *New York Times*, April 28, 1977, p. A12.

103. See the account in *Russkaia mysl'*, October 5, 1978, p. 9.

104. On VSKhSON, see John B. Dunlop, *The New Russian Revolutionaries* (Belmont, Mass.: Nordland, 1976).

105. Evgenii Vagin, "O monarkhicheskikh nastroeniiakh v sovetskoi Rossii." A clipping of this article, which appeared in *Nasha strana* (Buenos Aires), was sent to me without the date of publication being indicated. Internal evidence suggests that it appeared in the period October–December, 1976.

106. Iu. Kublanovskii, "Iz tserkovnoi storozhki," *Russkaia mysl'*, February 3, 1983.

107. Ibid. On the canonization of the imperial family by the

Russian Church Abroad, see "A New St. Nicholas for the Russians," *Time*, November 16, 1981, p. 63.

108. Kublanovskii, "Iz tserkovnoi storozhki."

109. Evgenii Evtushenko, "Iagodnye mesta," *Moskva* 10 (1981): 3-123 and 11 (1981): 52-111. This novel has appeared in an English translation by Antonia Bouis: *Wild Berries* (New York: Morrow, 1984).

110. Ibid., 10 (1981): 121.

111. On the "essayist" as a composite figure, see Sergei Iur'-enen, "Vladimir Soloukhin: Reabilitatsiia s voznagrazhdeniem," Radio Liberty Research Paper, RS 133/84, June 26, 1984, pp. 2-3.

112. On this film, see N. Kovarskii, "Sud istorii," *Iskusstvo kino* 12 (1965): 11-16. Former Duma leader Vasilii Shul'gin lived an extraordinary life: born in 1878, in the reign of Alexander II, he died a decade into Brezhnev's period of rule (in 1976). An émigré in Yugoslavia during the 1920s and 1930s, Shul'gin was arrested by Soviet forces during World War II and spent more than 10 years in prison before being released, ahead of sentence, in 1956. Taking up residence in the ancient Russian town of Vladimir, Shul'gin then served as a magnet for those interested in the reign of Russia's last tsar (among others, Mark Kasvinov and Nikolai Iakovlev made the pilgrimage and interviewed Shul'gin extensively). Shul'gin's mind reportedly remained lucid until the end and his monarchist and Russian nationalist convictions, firm and unchanged. In 1965, he was permitted, in collaboration with journalist Vladimir Vladimirov, to narrate a film entitled "Before the Judgment of History," which treated Nicholas II's reign. The two also collaborated on a book of memoirs, *Gody* (Years), which was published by Novosti in 1979. Shul'gin's program, if one can call it that, seems to be reasonably clear. He advocates the "Franco path" to a restoration of monarchy, to be effected not through civil war, which would be catastrophic, but in the "Old Russian" way – by a coup. The new Stolypin or Stolypins should steer clear of the shoals of racism and mindless reaction while seeking to regenerate the country through vigorous social and economic reform.

113. *New York Times*, November 8, 1981, p. 8E.

114. For the screenplay on which this film was based, see *Iskusstvo kino* 7 (1967): 119-160. See also the review of the film by M. Zak in *Iskusstvo kino* 11 (1968): 19-23. (After completing this article, I became acquainted with Yuliya Voznesenskaya's interesting "Transformation of the Image of the White Guard Of-

ficer in Soviet Cinema," Radio Liberty Research Paper, RL 409/84, October 23, 1984.)

115. Evgenii Vagin, "Pravda ob ubiistve tsarskoi sem'i," *Veche: Nezavisimyi russkii al'manakh* 4 (1982); 188. Italics in original.

116. A. I. Udodov, "Desiat' let v sovetskikh lageriakh," *Chasovoi* 12 (1975).

117. Andrei Korzhinskii, "Ofitsery," *Posev* 8 (1984): 27.

118. The reference is probably to Mikhail Bulgakov's novel *The White Guard* and to his play based on the novel, *Days of the Turbins*. Although these works have been published in the Soviet Union, they have appeared in a quantity completely inadequate to satisfy the demand.

119. The Golitsyns and Obolenskiis are, of course, two of the oldest and most distinguished Russian princely families.

120. "Otkrytoe pis'mo uchastnikam Belogo dvizheniia," *Posev* 11 (1983): 33–34.

121. Mikhail Gol'dshtein, "Zametki o monarkhicheskikh nastroniiakh v SSSR," *Vozrozhdenie* 242 (1973): 118.

122. "K budushchei svobodnoi Rossii" (interview with Evgenii Vagin), *Russkaia mysl'*, January 18, 1979, p. 7.

123. The term is Lenin's. It is also the title of a useful survey of Soviet and East European film of the post-Stalin period: Mira and Antonin Liehm, *The Most Important Art* (Berkeley, Calif.: University of California Press, 1977). For an important recent Soviet decree on film, see "V Tsentral'nom Komitete KPSS i Sovete Ministrov SSSR," *Pravda*, May 6, 1984, pp. 1–2.

124. An example of this "traditional" approach would be the volume, *The Soviet Union Today*, edited by James Cracraft and published by the *Bulletin of the Atomic Scientists* in 1983. The book contains two good chapters on Soviet literature and one survey of the cultural scene, but makes only a single reference to film.

125. These figures were provided by Andrei Mikhalkov-Konchalovskii during a lecture given at Oberlin College in 1983. He stated that the figures had been published in official Soviet sources. One should note that these figures refer to paying customers. Films that have been endorsed by the government and shown in schools, factories, etc., have enjoyed higher attendance. For examples of such films, see the reports of F.T. Ermash, the chairman of Goskino, in *Iskusstvo kino* 7 (1978): 20, and of his deputy, M. Aleksandrov, in *Iskusstvo kino* 8 (1979): 103–104.

126. "Pochemu tak vzvolnovany zriteli? (Kruglyi stol 'IK')," *Isskustvo kino* 9 (1980): 33. Surkov was replaced as the journal's editor in mid-1982.

127. "V kakoi elektrichke edet Gosha?" *Sovetskii ekran* 13 (1980): 14–15. *Sovetskii ekran* conducts an annual poll of its readers which can be of certain limited use to sociologists of film.

128. "Pochemu tak vzvolnovany . . . ," 28.

129. Ibid., 16.

130. Ibid., 14.

131. Ibid., 35.

132. Ibid., 18.

133. Ibid.

134. Ibid., 24.

135. Ibid., 26.

136. See note 127 for reference.

137. "Pochemu tak vzvolnovany . . . ," 25.

138. Ibid., 30.

139. Ibid.

140. Ibid., 31.

141. The theme of the "anthill" is, of course, a leitmotif in Dostoevskii's *Notes from Underground.*

142. *People*, April 11, 1983, p. 38.

143. For reviews of the film, see *Isskustvo kino* 9 (1979): 24–41, and *Sovetskii ekran* 17 (1979): 2–4. As far as I am aware, no roundtable discussion of *Siberiade* was organized by the authorities.

144. Mehnert, *The Russians and Their Favorite Books*, 215.

145. Ibid., 218.

146. The hymn "Many Years" is sung in the Orthodox Church on festive occasions such as a parishioner's name day or the anniversary of the ordination of a priest.

147. Keston College has reasonably complete copies of both issues.

148. G.M. Shimanov, "Lie Abramson," II, p. 153. Here and subsequently, the roman numeral I refers to the 1980 almanac, while II refers to the 1981 issue.

149. G.M. Shimanov, "Demokraticheskoe pravosoznanie," I, p. 63.

150. Ibid., 73.

151. Ibid., 72.

152. Ibid., 66.

153. Shimanov, "Lie Abramson," II, p. 146.

154. Shimanov, "Demokraticheskoe pravosoznanie," I, p. 65.

155. Shimanov, "Lie Abramson," II, p. 148. In general, Shimanov's comments on the United States demonstrate the power of the half-truth.

156. Shimanov, "Demokraticheskoe pravosoznanie," I, pp. 67–68.

157. Ibid., 73.

158. Ibid., 74.

159. Ibid., 76. Italics in original.

160. Shimanov, "Lie Abramson," p. 161.

161. "Pis'mo sviashchenniku Aleksandru Meniu," I, p. 227. Italics in original.

162. Ibid., 218.

163. Ibid., 219.

164. F.V. Karelin, "Teologicheskii manifest," II, p. 35.

165. V. Ibragimov, "Anatomiia velikoi mistifikatsii," I, p. 202.

166. Ibid., 186.

167. Ibid., 202.

168. F.V. Karelin, "Dva svidetel'stva," II, p. 25.

169. Shimanov, "Lie Abramson," II, p. 144.

170. Ibid., 142.

171. Shimanov, "Demokraticheskoe samosoznanie," I, p. 69.

172. Karelin, "Teologicheskii manifest," II, p. 23.

173. Ibid., 35.

174. Ibid., 26.

175. Karelin, "Dva svidetel'stva," I, p. 24.

176. Ibid., 38.

177. Discussed in Karelin, "Teologicheskii manifest," 2–3.

178. Karelin, "Dva svidetel'stva," I, p. 53.

179. Ibid., 56.

180. Ibid., 43.

181. "Sergeiu I . . . vu," I, p. 84.

182. Ibid.

183. Karelin, "Dva svidetel'stva," I, p. 46.

184. Shimanov, "Lie Abramson," II, p. 144.

185. V. Ibragimov, "Nazyvaia fakty," II, pp. 71–72.

186. Karelin, "Teologicheskii manifest," II, p. 35.

187. A. I. Kazakov, "Istoki i korni," II, p. 126.

188. Shimanov, "Lie Abramson," II, p. 160.

189. Ibid., 159.

190. Shimanov writes in "To Leah Abramson": ". . . . both the

peoples of Russia and Slavs abroad (and perhaps not only Slavs) will, it seems, take their geographic and historical ties to Rus' into consideration. . . . " II, p. 156.

191. Ibid.

192. V. N. Trostnikov, "Sud'by liudskie," II, p. 46.

193. T. Chernysheva, "Russkaia krasota," II, pp. 78–80.

194. For the text of one such piece of legislation, see U.S. Congress, *Religious Persecution in the Soviet Union: Hearings before the Subcommittees on International Political and Military Affairs and on International Organizations of the Committee on International Relations, House of Representatives*, 94th Cong., 1st sess., June 24 and 30, 1976.

195. Konrad Adenauer, *Memoirs 1945–53* (Chicago, Ill.: Henry Regnery Company, 1966), 39.

196. The fourteenth century Byzantine theologians systematized a tradition that went back to the apostolic church and the Desert Fathers. On this subject, one could cite the writings of Russian émigré theologians Georges Florovsky, Vladimir Lossky, and John Meyendorff. For the hesychast tradition in Russia, see my study *Staretz Amvrosy*, 17–38.

197. See Vladimir Soloukhin, *Vremia sobirat' kamni: Ocherki* (Moscow: "Sovremennik," 1980), 169–234.

198. See the appendix to the 1981 almanac: Fedor Abramov's "Iz kolena Avvakumova."

199. V. Ibragimov, "Anatomiia velikoi mistifikatskii," I, p. 159.

200. In response to a personal query from me, delivered through an intermediary.

201. "Litsom k Rossii: Interv'iu E. A. Vagina 'Posevu'", *Posev* 10 (1976): 58.

202. Sergei Semanov, *Serdtse rodiny* (Moscow: "Moskovskii rabochii," 1977).

203. Ibid., 163.

204. Nikolai Iakovlev, *1 avgusta 1914* (Moscow, *Molodaia gvardiia*, 1974); Valentin Pikul', "U poslednei cherty" in *Nash sovremennik*, nos. 4–7, 1979.

205. "La Technique du Pouvoir en URSS" (An interview with Alain Besançon), *L'Express*, December 2–9, 1978, p. 92.

206. Michel Tatu believes the the USSR "may be a military dictatorship by the end of the century—possibly by the end of the decade." *Newsweek*, November 22, 1982, p. 42. And Jerry Hough

reports that there are "major American specialists" who privately predict a military dictatorship in the Soviet Union. Jerry F. Hough, "Soviet Succession: Issues and Personalities," *Problems of Communism* (September–October 1982), 27. A military dictatorship, as distinct from a KGB-dominated dictatorship, would be likely to have a Russian nationalist coloration.